# Think & Grow Balls!

How To Shrink Your Fear & Enlarge Your Courage

A Guide For Motivating and Encouraging You To Reach Your Escape Velocity

By:  J.D. Bloodstone

ISBN: 978-0-557-18360-9

## The Bad Guy Notice

# Acknowledgments

I would like to thank life for providing me with an unfair playing field and the "he-bitch, man-slaps" I needed to rid myself of my inflated ego, stubbornness, arrogance, and forcing me to try harder. At the same time, I would also like to thank life for allowing me to understand the rules of the game, allowing me to develop my own strategy, and allowing me to select my own opponents and teammates so that I might be able to tip the scales in my favor. I also thank life for making me work for the things I have and for taking away the things I am given. This book is a testament to what I have learned. Life may not want me sharing my ideas with everyone else, but I'm going to do it anyway. See you on the flipside.

I thank Napoleon Hill for writing *Think & Grow Rich*, and my father for lending me his copy.

I thank my mother and grandmother for seeing my potential and convincing others of it. It's fair to say my life would be VERY different had it not been for their interventions.

# Table of Contents

# Foreword

*"Assume a virtue, if you have it not."* – William Shakespeare

## Why an e-Book on "Balls"?

First, what are "balls"? Or, better yet, what is "balls"? And, what does it mean to have them? No, I'm not talking about testicles or any spherical objects used in sporting events or other physical activities. I'm talking about assumption, assurance, audacity, backbone, boldness, brass, bravery, brazenness, cheek, chutzpah, cajones, confidence, coolness, courage, crust, determination, effrontery, endurance, energy, face, fearlessness, firmness, force, fortitude, gall, gameness, grit, guts, hardihood, hardiness, heart, impertinence, impudence, intestinal fortitude, intrepidity, melons, mettle, might, moxie, pluck, presumption, resolution, sauce, spirit, spunk, starch, steadfastness, stomach, temerity, vigor, and will. I'm talking about the character trait that separates winners from losers and "the men from the boys". I'm talking about being able to look fear or a seemingly impossible task in the eye and jump in anyway. This is what I mean by the term "balls". And, we admire those individuals that prove to us they have them, even if it means their demise.

So, why did I write an e-book on "balls"? The short answer is: because the world desperately NEEDS it. There are countless authors writing great books and putting together wonderful programs on how to do everything from buying real estate with no money down, placing ads in classified newspapers around the country, starting a home-based business, to buying and selling on eBay. And, yet, the majority of people that purchase self-help and self-improvement materials NEVER DO ANYTHING with the materials they have paid a lot of hard-earned money for. Why is that? Well, as Morpheus put it in the movie, *The Matrix*, "Knowing the path, is different from walking the path". Simply put, ALL THE KNOWLEDGE AND INFORMATION IN THE WORLD IS NOT ENOUGH TO MAKE YOU

WEALTHY, HEALTHY, OR SUCCESSFUL; YOU MUST ACTUALLY DO SOMETHING WITH THE KNOWLEDGE IN ORDER TO GET RESULTS IN YOUR LIFE. That's right, you actually have to have the "balls" to take action... to roll the dice... to take your chances.

So, how is this e-book different from what's already available? Ah, good question. This e-book is different because I'm not going to rehash anything you may have previously read on improving your life and I'm not going to tell you how you can make $30,000 in one month by selling cheap items from drop-ship merchandisers. I'm going to teach you the formula on how to develop your action-oriented power attitude so you may apply it to any aspect of your life that you choose. And, if you CHOOSE to apply your new power attitude to your life, I will make you a promise... you will become action-oriented and you will wield power. More importantly, people in your life will perceive you as such and treat you differently.

Over the years, I have read printed books, listened to countless audio books, and sat through hours of DVD programs. I learned from anything I could get my hands on that dealt with the power of thought to reprogram our subconscious minds in order to bring about and attract more success, wealth, and happiness to our lives. I couldn't get enough of them.

Several years ago, I borrowed a copy of *Think & Grow Rich*, by Napoleon Hill, from my father, and I realized I had hit the jackpot and located the source from which ALL self-help and self-improvement material flows. I had stumbled across the very formula for success in life and for the first time in a long time, I had found a sense of profound peace and yet, at the same time, a burning desire had awakened in me to learn all I could about Napoleon Hill and his work.

After spending <u>thousands of dollars</u> and countless days of learning, absorbing, and testing, I can tell you that *Think & Grow Rich* is the real thing. In fact, it is so powerful, that EVERY self-help guru who has ever lived (during and after Napoleon Hill's life) and had a self-help product on the market accredits their success and powerful outlook on life to Napoleon Hill, W. Clement Stone, or Jack Canfield (for the record, W. Clement Stone was Napoleon Hill's apprentice and Jack Canfield was W. Clement Stone's apprentice, so invariably they are all teaching the EXACT SAME philosophy). Sometimes, these gurus will name all three of these men, or two, or just one in the acknowledgement sections of their works. But here's the catch: they are ALL restating the same concepts and retelling the same stories (just with the dates and names changed for modernization) to get their slice of the pie that Napoleon Hill originally baked.

Here's my question to you? Wouldn't it be exciting and refreshing for one of these gurus to take this information to the next level? Wouldn't it be nice for someone with mastery of this subject to show you how to apply this powerful mindset to your life and PUT IT INTO ACTION? This might be more than you can chew right now (especially if this is the first time you're being introduced to Napoleon Hill's philosophy), so let me explain what I mean. According to the publisher, *Think & Grow Rich* has sold more than 60 million copies worldwide. If this is true, and Napoleon Hill's philosophy is so powerful and life changing, why are there 59,999,900 readers (this is a figure I conjured up but hopefully you'll get my point) still in the same place in their lives as they were before they picked up their copy? Now, add to that all the hundreds of clone books and materials written by Napoleon Hill's army and you get an even larger number of people that, although enchanted by the philosophy, ARE STILL DOING THE SAME THINGS WITH THEIR LIVES. Why is this? Is something missing in the recipe for Napoleon Hill's original pie? Is an entire chapter missing from his work? Did Mr. Hill leave out a crucial piece of his success formula? I believe he did. The missing chapter or piece is on "balls" and that YOU MUST SUMMON THE COURAGE TO TAKE ACTION IN YOUR LIFE, and no one, not even Mr. Hill, has ever given you the formula for developing balls and taking the chance on making your life the way you want it. If I'm successful in this e-book, you'll have the formula to do anything you want in your life.

I must confess, when I first began doing my research and jotting down my notes for the first draft of this e-book, I had intended it to be for men only; however, during the course of my field research with people of both genders, I found that BOTH MEN AND WOMEN WERE USING THE WORD "BALLS" IN EXACTLY THE SAME WAY. (In one particular case, I heard a woman reference herself as having more balls than many men she meets and that this was sad because she doesn't even have real ones.) In fact, it was the veracity of its use by women that made me rethink my audience for this e-book to include everyone. Although perhaps coined by men, the word "balls", which originally expressed an ideal of manhood (or the lack thereof), has clearly risen above the confines of the sexes and is now a common and humorous word to describe a personality trait that WE ALL DESIRE.

Even if you've never been introduced to any of Napoleon Hill's works or those of any of his followers, this will still be of priceless value to you (I highly recommend going out and purchasing and reading the 21st-Century Edition of *Think & Grow Rich* if you can). Consider yourself lucky that you are the first to get the missing piece to the personal power puzzle... from start to finish... and beyond. I give you, THINK & GROW BALLS!

# Introduction

"Be a Columbus to whole new continents and worlds within you, opening new channels, not of trade, but of thought." – Henry David Thoreau

## Behind the Philosophy

I think that in order to be responsible in the writing of this material I need to state this early on... I believe that all humans are unique and different from one another... spiritually.

And, yet, I believe we are all born with similar physical systems and functions that we are able to use in perceiving, interpreting, comprehending, and responding to our lives and environment if we choose.  To be specific, I believe all of us to have neurotransmitters (i.e., amino acids, peptides, and monoamines) that carry signals (energy) to our central nervous system (brain and spinal cord) and our peripheral nervous system (limbs and organs) to help us experience our lives.  These signals cause glands and organs in our bodies to release a myriad of chemical compounds that regulate the functionality and safety of our bodies (e.g., hormones) that act as messengers that carry signals from one cell (or groups of cells) to another.  And, since I believe our bodies to be a system, the chemical compounds in turn influence the brain and the cycle starts all over again, with one system affecting the other... over and over and over again.

I believe that within our brains resides the entity that we call our "psyche" or "mind" which in turn houses all thoughts and their correlating processes.  I BELIEVE THE WAY WE THINK IS A HABIT OR A PATTERN OF THE PSYCHE OR MIND THAT WE CAN ENTIRELY CONTROL (for better or for worse) if we choose to believe we can and take the appropriate steps to make it work for us.  For example, as you are reading this, there are thoughts (or a voice) responding to this material; those thoughts are generated by your mind and it is the functionality of your brain that is allowing you to speak silently and to hear your inner voice (or voices if you subscribe to Carl Jung's Complex of the Mind Theory).

Now, if your mind can control the physical activity of your brain and spinal cord, which according to modern science and technological breakthroughs we know to be true (i.e., MRIs and brain scans) then our mind can control the rest of our body (i.e., peripheral nervous system).

If your mind controls the systems of our body, then your mind is controlling the way we perceive, interpret, comprehend, and respond to your life and the environment you live in. And, if that's true... your mind is in control of your life... and, if you can control your mind (e.g., autosuggestion, meditation, etc.) you can therefore control your life. I know, that's pretty deep, but bear with me.

This e-book deals with one simple, yet complex idea: that your mind controls your brain and that it is in control of the release of chemical compounds (e.g., hormones) in your body that entirely dictate how you feel and often how you act. I posit that if you can control your mind through thought and condition them properly (habit of thought), you can control how your body responds to the natural chemicals of the body (both positive and negative), thus controlling how you feel (mind over matter). If you can do that, then you can predict with higher accuracy how you will act.

If you act in certain ways (i.e., confidently and self-assured... or powerful), then you will be perceived as confident, self-assured, and powerful. If you are perceived as such (through your body language and behavior), you will be treated as such, and these interactions with society and your environment will help affirm and reaffirm to your mind that you have power. And, since your physical body acts as a system, this behavior will send powerful signals through your entire body which will send signals back to the brain and repeat this process over and over and over again (this is why you must always "think happy thoughts" and "find your happy place"; because how you think causes your body to respond or to "make you feel" and experience emotions that can dictate how you act and are perceived and ultimately picked up by your mind and the process starts all over again).

I'd like to begin the remainder of this introduction with a quote: "Courage is not the absence of fear, but rather the judgment that something else is more important" by Ambrose Redmoon. I believe this quote holds much importance to the message behind this e-book: WE ALL FEEL FEAR AND ARE AFRAID AT TIMES, IT COMES WITH THE TERRITORY OF BEING HUMAN; HOWEVER, IT IS THE PROCESS OF THINKING THAT ENABLES US TO PERCEIVE AND DECIDE WHETHER THE REWARD OF ACTION OVERRIDES THE CONSEQUENCE OF NONACTION OR VICE VERSA.

Now, if you can reduce your mind's response to fear or change your mind's perception of it, you can reduce your body's response to fear. If you do that, you'll reduce the influence fear has on your decision-making abilities. In other words, if you are less influenced by fear, the actions and behaviors associated with courage (i.e., balls) will be easier to perform. The more you do them, the more they get engrained in your subconscious minds to become habit. Once these actions and behaviors become habit they will seem easier and more natural. This is where your power-attitude comes in; but, before you go down the path of power, you must first understand how your mind and body work together to help you experience life efficiently. Before I do that, though, I'd like to introduce you to Napoleon Hill and his masterpiece *Think & Grow Rich*.

# STAGE ONE

"Happy are those who dream dreams and are ready to pay the price to make them come true." – Leon J. Suenes

# The Engine

"Whatever the mind of man can conceive and believe it can achieve."
- Napoleon Hill


## A Brief Introduction & Summary of *Think & Grow Rich*

I've heard it said that if you can't say something better than someone who already has, it's better if you quote him or her. To that extent, the following excerpt comes from *Think & Grow Rich*, by Napoleon Hill:

> "[Napoleon Hill] …was assigned to write a profile of the famed steel baron Andrew Carnegie. Their three-hour interview turned into a three-day marathon. It concluded with Carnegie proposing that he would introduce Hill to the most powerful men in America so that Hill could learn from them their secrets of success. But he would do so only if Hill agreed to use those secrets to write a philosophy of success that would be made available to, and could be understood by, the average person.

> Napoleon Hill accepted Andrew Carnegie's offer on the spot, and thus was granted the rare opportunity to study firsthand the greatest business leaders in the world including Henry Ford, Thomas Edison, Harvey Firestone, Alexander Graham Bell, John D. Rockefeller Jr., the Wright Brothers, F.W. Woolworth, Luther Burbank, Marshall Field, and hundreds more.

> Andrew Carnegie also arranged for Hill to meet President Theodore Roosevelt and President William Howard Taft, and both President Woodrow Wilson and President Franklin D. Roosevelt asked Hill to work for them when they served in the White House. Mahatma Gandhi sought him out, as did other world leaders and heads of state.

For almost thirty years Napoleon Hill devoted himself to interviewing over five hundred of the most famous and successful leaders in every field, as well as thousands of other entrepreneurs, both successes and failures. The result of those years of exhaustive research made Hill one of the best-selling authors in history and one of the most influential voices in America."

In *Think & Grow Rich*, Napoleon Hill lists thirteen traits, or principles, that all successful people must possess (or already possess) and suggests methods on how to acquire and develop them. The thirteen traits and their brief descriptions are given below:

Desire – Knowing EXACTLY what you want and what you will give in return for its attainment.

Faith – Unshakable belief in yourself and your ability to obtain the object of your desire.

Autosuggestion – Influencing and directing your subconscious mind towards the attainment of your desire by self-suggesting positive and dominating thoughts to yourself at least twice a day; and doing it with such conviction that you trigger emotions or feelings inside you.

Specialized Knowledge – Knowledge of the service, merchandise, or profession that you intend to offer in return for the attainment of your desire.

Imagination – Engaging your "synthesizing" and "creative" abilities to help turn your desire into its physical counterpart.

Organized Planning – Making practical plans that include the cooperation of others to help obtain the object of your desire.

Decision – The habit of reaching decisions promptly, and of changing these decisions slowly.

<u>Persistence</u> – Pushing past failures until you reach the object of your desire.

<u>Power of the Master Mind</u> – Tapping into and acquiring greater knowledge through infinite intelligence, accumulated experience, and experiments and research.

<u>Sexuality</u> – Redirecting your sexual energy and the need for its expression towards the attainment of your desire, rather than letting it distract you, so you can develop charisma and creativity.

<u>The Subconscious Mind</u> – Understanding that you can use your conscious mind to (1) plant any plan, thought, or purpose to program your subconscious mind, until it becomes a habit, and (2), open your subconscious mind to infinite intelligence to evoke positive emotions and feelings to help transform your desire into concrete form.

<u>The Brain</u> – Understanding that just like the principle behind the operation of a radio transmitter and receiver, every human brain is capable of sending and picking up vibrations of human thought to and from other brains (hunches and intuitions).

<u>The Sixth Sense</u> – Knowing that after the other twelve principles have been mastered, you can use your subconscious mind to receive signals from infinite intelligence to warn you of impending dangers in time to avoid them, notify you of opportunities in time to take advantage of them, and to tap the source of inspiration.

Along with the thirteen principles of his success philosophy, Napoleon Hill lists the six basic fears that, either one by one, or in some combination, stand in the way and keep a person from being successful.  He calls these six fears "The Six Ghosts of Fear" and he lists them in order of their most common appearance and the potential damage they do to those inflicted (they need little to no explanation):

The Fear of Poverty
The Fear of Criticism

The Fear of Ill Health
The Fear of Loss of Love of Someone
The Fear of Old Age
The Fear of Death


I'm not going to elaborate on the ghosts of fear (as I do not want to focus my thoughts on them) and I'm not going to dive deeper into the meanings and applications of the thirteen principles of Mr. Hill's success philosophy. I'm only going to, once again, recommend that if this philosophy intrigues you, you should pick up the 21st-Century Edition of *Think & Grow Rich*. I bet you it'll be worth it!

If you have read it, read it again. Brush up. THE PROCESS OF MASTERY GUARANTEES THAT EVERY TIME YOU READ IT, YOU'LL PICK UP SOMETHING NEW OR SEE SOMETHING YOU THOUGHT YOU KNEW IN A DIFFERENT WAY.

At this time, I'd like you to reexamine the list of principles Napoleon Hill lists as required (or as already acquired) and tell me if you see "Balls" anywhere? Go ahead, I'll wait for you.

Good. You're back. Don't you think that "COURAGE TO TAKE ACTION" (or some variation thereof) should be on this list? I certainly do. I've even read Napoleon Hill's other great works, including his ultimate masterpiece, Law of Success, (also the 21st-Century Edition) which is so robust it was originally published in four volumes. Even in this 1,000 plus page tome on how to achieve success he doesn't mention that IT ALSO TAKES CAJONES OR BALLS TO EVEN TAKE THE FIRST STEP TOWARDS SUCCESS. To be fair, I think he dances around the issue; touching it here and there. But, he never actually addresses it. Here's what I think: the people who have been inspired to achieve success by Napoleon Hill's work already had the balls to take action towards achieving their object of desire. For those individuals that don't have balls, however, he leaves you with an amazing burning desire in your gut with no way to express it or act on it. That is why I set out to write this e-book. I think "Balls" should be a principle in Napoleon Hill's philosophy (and everyone else's, for that matter), but it's not. So, I had to write it.

From here, I think I can go deeper into my own philosophy on how you can acquire and develop your own balls and your own courage to take action. But, before I do, there are a few concepts that I must teach you to build your foundation. I'll do that now in the next chapters.

It's time to THINK & GROW BALLS!

# Fuel

"The subjective mind is entirely under the control of the objective mind.  With the utmost fidelity it reproduces and works out to it final consequences whatever the objective mind impresses on it." –
Thomas Troward

## Your Conscious & Subconscious Mind

Most people in today's day in age believe in the concept of "the mind".  Not the brain... which is physical, but, the mind... where all thought occurs.  I'm going to broaden the definition a little and say that the mind is the center of your self-esteem, or what you BELIEVE to be true about your self-worth, your environment and your place within it, and your purpose.

Modern psychology has shown that the mind has two distinct parts, each with its own function and purpose.  These two parts are known as the conscious and the subconscious mind.  Without these to parts of our mind working together to enable you to perceive, interpret, decide, and respond to your surroundings, you would not have the life you currently have.  In fact, all human life would be different.

Carl Jung, one of the founding fathers of modern psychology, suggested that the conscious and subconscious minds fit together like an iceberg.  The conscious mind represents the tip of the iceberg above the water line that you and the world can "see".  The subconscious mind represents the huge mass of the iceberg below the water line and out of view from yourself and the world.  The tip of the iceberg, or conscious, makes up 10% of our total mind while the unseen mass beneath the surface, or subconscious, makes up 90%.

The conscious mind, representing the smallest part of our mind, is where you "live" while you perceive, interpret, decide, and respond to your surroundings.  YOUR CONSCIOUS MIND ALWAYS LIVES IN THE PRESENT.  EVEN IF YOU ENGAGE IT TO RECALL PAST EVENTS OR FUTURE POSSIBILITIES YOUR CONSCIOUS MIND IS STILL WORKING WITH WHAT IT BELIEVES TO BE TRUE AT THAT MOMENT.  Your internal voice, or the voice you use to speak to yourself also lives in your conscious mind.  This is commonly referred to as your Ego.  It is your self.

The subconscious mind, representing the largest part of our mind, is out of view, or under the surface, and even though we can't see it, it plays a huge part in guiding our conscious mind.  The concept of the subconscious mind and what it does has long been argued; however, both medicine and psychology recognize that it exists.

I believe the subconscious mind is the repository of the sum total of all your experiences during your life.  It absorbs your conscious thoughts, one by one, and systematically categorizes them to be stored and called upon later by the conscious mind.  I believe this is done for a good reason... TO MAKE YOUR CONSCIOUS MIND MORE EFFICIENT IN WHATEVER TASKS YOU DIRECT YOUR BODY TOWARD.  Think about it this way.  Imagine all the incoming data that is bombarding your brain during every second of your waking life.  If you combine the signals your brain is receiving via your five senses: sight, smell, touch, taste, and hearing, you start to realize that your brain is constantly on overload.  And, in order to continue to operate at the speed that your body and life require, your conscious mind must make judgments... it must assume... it must categorize... it must generalize... it has to survive.  Every second that passes causes billions of neurons in your brain to "fire", or send signals to other cells in your brain and body just in order to exist.  If the conscious mind dwelled on the information it takes in every second, then it wouldn't be able to process the next second... or the next one... or the next one... and on and on again.  The conscious mind must make assessments and I believe the subconscious mind is where your conscious mind stores these assessments.

To use a modern analogy, you can think of your conscious mind as the Central Processing Unit (CPU) on the motherboard of a computer and Random Access Memory (RAM) modules as your subconscious. Just as a CPU's function is to process and calculate ONLY current tasks, so does your conscious mind. RAM's function is to store the results of the CPU's processes and calculations so the CPU can perform other tasks until the sums and results are needed and called upon to complete a current task. The function of RAM is the same as the function of the subconscious mind.

RAM memory is erased each time you turn off or reboot your computer. In fact, the reason why it takes so long to boot your computer is because the CPU must reprocess and recalculate every present function in turning itself on and rewriting the RAM so it is capable of performing the tasks you command it to. Your brain does not have that ability... nor do I think you'd want it to.

Now, imagine your subconscious mind as RAM that never gets erased... never gets rebooted or turned off. Imagine what your subconscious must do over your lifespan. Can you imagine that as time passes your subconscious mind "fills up" or becomes "saturated" with sums and conclusions that your conscious mind has calculated over your lifespan? What does it do now? I believe that, eventually, your subconscious mind makes sums of sums... it generalizes generalities... it categorizes categories... it assumes assumptions; IT CREATES A NEW LEVEL OF SUBCONSCIOUS UNDERSTANDING, as I like to call it. I believe this is what's happening when you experience de ja vu, those "ah-ha" moments, or when you have an epiphany or a paradigm shift. Your subconscious mind has reached a new level of understanding. It's downshifting.

I don't believe this process ever ends. Eventually, if you live long enough OR ARE EXPOSED TO AN EQUIVALENT AMOUNT OF INFORMATION, your subconscious mind will make sums of sums of sums... and will generalize generalities of generalities... and will... you get the picture.

If we understand the subconscious mind in this way, we can finally begin to realize how habits work, both good ones and bad ones, and why they're so hard to break. Because you must "REPROGRAM" your subconscious mind so that the sums and conclusions that make up its core are the sums and conclusions that you want your conscious mind to have access to while it calculates and concludes in the present.

YOU DON'T GET TO TURN OFF OR REBOOT YOUR MIND SO WE MUST WORK THOUGHTS IN GRADUALLY.

I believe the subconscious mind is impartial. I don't believe it has the ability to comprehend right from wrong or good from bad. I believe it only records and categorizes what the conscious mind told it to at the exact time the conscious mind made its impression on the subconscious mind.

So... BE CAREFUL WHAT YOU THINK AND SAY TO YOURSELF!!! Your subconscious mind is always recording and categorizing.

I'm going to take this theory one step further and expand the concept of your conscious and subconscious mind to how your entire body functions.

Your physical movements and actions in the present are controlled by your conscious mind... meaning that if you think of doing something you can do it now if you choose. The other movements or processes by your body (e.g., digestion, perspiration, fight-or-flight response, breathing, eye blinking, tear secretion, hair and nail growth, aging of the body, organ functions, etc.) are controlled by your subconscious mind... meaning that you DON'T have think about these things in order to do them. They're automatic and part of your central nervous system.

I believe your subconscious mind controls your central nervous system too. And, this includes your sympathetic and parasympathetic nervous system. These two systems are what regulate your hormone and neurotransmitter levels in your body. And, I BELIEVE YOU CAN PROGRAM YOUR SUBCONSCIOUS MIND TO CONTROL (OR AT LEAST HELP CONTROL) THESE TWO SYSTEMS TO

WORK IN WAYS THAT BENEFIT YOU.  I BELIEVE THAT IF YOU DO, YOU CAN CONTROL HOW YOU FEEL.

In this e-book, I'm going to specifically talk about the emotion of fear, how you comprehend it and the effect that it has on your body. Why I'm doing this is an overarching idea of my theory: if you reduce your conscious and subconscious reaction or response to fear, acts and deeds of courage (i.e., balls) will be easier to perform.  Now, on to the next chapter.

# Reaction

"Our doubts are traitors, and make us lose the good we oft might win by fearing to attempt." – William Shakespeare

I discuss fear and the fight-or-flight response in this e-book because I want to expose this emotion and its effect on your body for what it truly is... something common, natural, powerful, AND COMPLETELY UNDER YOUR CONTROL!

All you have to do is recognize fear when it overtakes you, understand the message it is sending to your body, and you will be half way to mastery!

Before you can recognize fear, you need to know what it is...

## Fear

According to Wikipedia.org, fear is defined as, "an emotional response to impending danger, that is tied to anxiety. Most fear is usually connected to pain." I believe this pain can be physical or psychological such as the fear of heights resulting in falling to your death or the fear of public speaking and making a mistake causing you to be embarrassed and judged negatively. Wikipedia.org goes on to say:

> Fear is a survival mechanism, and usually occurs in response to a specific negative stimulus.

> Serious fear is a response to some formidable impending peril, while trifling fear arises from confrontation with inconsequential danger.

Fear can be described by different terms in accordance with its relative degrees. Personal fear varies extremely in degree from mild caution to extreme phobia and paranoia. Fear is related to a number of emotional states including worry, anxiety, terror, fright, paranoia, horror, panic (social and personal), persecution complex, and dread.

Fears may be a factor within a larger social network, wherein personal fears are synergistically compounded as mass hysteria.

Although fear is an innate response (meaning we all have it and it happens naturally), OBJECTS OF FEAR CAN BE LEARNED (OR UNLEARNED I BELIEVE). This has been studied in psychology as fear conditioning, beginning with Watson's Little Albert experiment in 1920. In this study, an 11-month-old boy was conditioned to fear a white rat in the laboratory. In the real world, fear may also be acquired by a traumatic accident. For example, if a child falls into a well and struggles to get out, he or she may develop a fear of wells, enclosed spaces (claustrophobia) or of water (hydrophobia).

Researchers have found that certain fears (e.g., animals and heights) are much more common that others (e.g., flowers and clouds) and are also much easier to induce in the laboratory. This phenomenon has been called "preparedness". (In other words, if fear is a survival mechanism and we are all capable of experiencing fear, then we as humans are born better "prepared" to deal with and survive certain common conditions versus other less common ones).

While fear is most commonly associated with physical conditions or objects, in humans, fear can also be inspired by more abstract concepts. The fear of losing control, for example, is a commonly referenced condition, as is fear of ridicule or social censure. These types of fear tend not to have the same physiological effects as fears of the more immediate physical world; however, they have similar behavioral outcomes, and can affect an individual on a far longer timescale that would typically be expected of a fear of a physical object.

(This next part is important, so pay close attention)

Philosopher Jiddu Krishnamurti said that, "thinking is the root cause of fear. Thinking about a painful incident in the past projects the fear of having the pain repeated again in the future. Fear is also related to pleasure. Thinking with the images of past pleasure, thought imagines that one may not have that pleasure repeated in the future; so thought engenders fear. Thought tries to sustain pleasure and thereby nourishes fear."

In fear, one may go through various emotional stages. A good example of this is the *cornered rat*, which will try to run away until it is finally cornered by its predator, at which point it will become belligerent and fight back with heavy aggression until it either escapes or is captured.

The same goes for most animals. Humans can become very intimidated by fear; causing them to go along with another's wishes without caring about their own input. They can also become equally violent, and can even become deadly; it is an instinctive reaction caused by rising adrenaline levels rather than a consciously thought-out decision (I believe this process to occur at the subconscious level of the brain).

The facial expression of fear includes the following components:

- One's eyes widen (out of anticipation for what will happen next)
- The pupils dilate (to take in more light)
- The upper lip rises
- The brows draw together
- Lips stretch horizontally

The physiological effects of fear can be better understood from the perspective of the sympathetic nervous responses (fight-or-flight):

- Muscles used for physical movement are tightened and primed with oxygen in preparation for a physical fight or flight response.
- Perspiration occurs due to blood being shunted from the body's viscera to the peripheral parts of the body. Blood that is shunted from the viscera to the rest of the body transfers oxygen, nutrients, and heat, prompting perspiration to cool itself.
- When the stimulus is shocking or abrupt, a common reaction is to cover or otherwise protect vulnerable parts of the anatomy, particularly the face and head.
- When a fear stimulus occurs unexpectedly, the victim of the fear response could possibly jump or give a small start.
- The person's heart rate is likely to increase.
- The person may also experience piloerection ("goose bumps" or hair standing on end).

Fear is the flip side of anger in the inbuilt human "fight or flight" response.

Even the legal system recognizes fear. The following is a passage from Wikipedia.org entry on fear and the law:

> The cause of fear is found in oneself or in a natural cause (intrinsic fear) or it is found in another person (extrinsic fear). Fear may be grave, such for instance as would influence a steadfast man, or it may be slight, such as would affect a person of weak will. In order that fear may be considered grave, certain conditions are requisite: the fear must be grave in itself, and not merely in the estimation of the person fearing; it must be based on a reasonable foundation; the threats must be possible of

execution; and the execution of the threats must be inevitable. Fear, again, is either just or unjust, according to the justness or otherwise of the reasons that lead to the use of fear as a compelling force. Reverential fear is that which may exist between superiors and their subjects. GRAVE FEAR DIMINISHES WILLPOWER BUT CANNOT BE SAID TO TOTALLY TAKE IT AWAY, EXCEPT IN SOME VERY EXCEPTIONAL CASES. Slight fear is not considered to diminish the will power, hence the legal expression, "foolish fear is not a just excuse."

Now, let's look at how fear manifests itself in your body...

## The Fight-or-Flight Response

Fear is the psychological trigger that causes the body to engage in a process that allows you to INSTANTANEOUSLY PERCEIVE AND JUDGE whether a stimulus in your life is a threat, and if so, how much of a threat does it pose. But more importantly, the process AUTOMATICALLY DICTATES how you will physically respond to the threat if one is PERCEIVED to exist. This process is known as the Fight-or-Flight Response and it happens in all vertebrate animals.

First described by Walter Cannon in 1915, the Fight-or-Flight Response (FOFR) theory states that animals react to threats with a general discharge of the sympathetic nervous system, priming the animal for fighting or fleeing. The FOFR is also called hyper-arousal or the acute stress response.

To better describe the biology of this response, I'm going to quote Wikipedia.org again (I apologize in advance for the technical jargon that is about to follow but the following passage explains this psychological and physical response far better than I ever could):

> Normally, when a person is in a serene, non-stimulated state, the "firing" of neurons in the locus ceruleus is minimal. A novel

stimulus (which could include a perception of danger or an environmental stresser signal such as elevated sound levels or over-illumination), once perceived, is relayed from the sensory cortex of the brain through the thalamus to the brain stem. That route of signaling increases the rate of noradrenergetic activity in the locus ceruleus, and the person becomes alert and attentive to the environment. Similarly, an abundance of catecholamines at neuroreceptor sites facilitates reliance on spontaneous or intuitive behaviors often related to combat or escape...

If a stimulus is perceived as a threat, a more intense and prolonged discharge of the locus ceruleus activates the sympathetic division of the autonomic nervous system (Thase & Howland, 1995). THIS ACTIVATION IS ASSOCIATED WITH SPECIFIC PHYSIOLOGICAL ACTIONS IN THE SYSTEM, BOTH DIRECTLY AND INDIRECTLY THROUGH THE RELEASE OF EPINEPHRINE (ADRENALINE) AND TO A LESSER EXTENT NOREPINEPHRINE FROM THE MEDULLA OF THE ADRENAL GLANDS. The release is triggered by acetylcholine released from preganglionic sympathetic nerves. The other major player in the acute stress response is the hypothalamic-pituitary-adrenal axis.

Now let's briefly look at the ways the FOFR manifests in the physical body:

- Acceleration of heart and lung action
- Inhibition of stomach and intestinal action
- Constriction of blood vessels in many parts of the body
- Liberation of nutrients for muscular action
- Dilation of blood vessels for muscles
- Inhibition of tear and saliva production
- Dilation of pupil
- Relaxation of bladder
- Inhibition of erection

In prehistoric times when the FOFR evolved in humans, fight was manifested in aggressive, combative behavior; flight was manifested by fleeing potentially threatening situations such as being confronted by a predator. In current times, these responses persist, but FOFRs have assumed a wider range of behaviors. For example, the fight response may be manifested in angry, argumentative behavior, and the flight response may be manifested through social withdrawal, substance abuse, and even television viewing. (Friedman & Silver 2007)

Although the emergency measure of the stress response is undoubtedly both vital and valuable, it can also be disruptive and damaging. IN MOST MODERN SITUATIONS, HUMANS RARELY ENCOUNTER EMERGENCIES THAT REQUIRE PHYSICAL EFFORT, YET OUR BIOLOGY STILL PROVIDES FOR THEM. Thus we may find our stress response activated in situations where physical action is inappropriate or even illegal. This activation takes a toll on both our bodies and our minds.

Disruption of the sexual response and the digestive system are common negative results. Diarrhea, constipation, and difficulty maintaining sexual arousal are typical examples. These are functions that are controlled by the parasympathetic nervous system and therefore suppressed by sympathetic arousal. Prolonged stress responses may result in chronic suppression of the immune system, leaving the sufferer vulnerable to infection by bacteria and viruses. Repeated stress responses can be caused not only by real threats, but also by mental disorders such as post-traumatic stress disorder, in which the individual shows a stress response when remembering a past trauma, and panic disorder, in which the stress response is activated apparently by nothing.

What I want you to take from this chapter on fear and the FOFR is that they are directly related to each other and that these responses are natural, innate, and occur automatically. Even more important, is that fear and the FOFR are completely responsible for the release of Epinephrine, commonly called adrenaline, and other related chemicals that enable you to respond to them either by some sort of aggressive behavior or by some sort of passive behavior. AND MOST IMPORTANTLY, IS THAT THIS EMOTION AND RESPONSE OCCURS BECAUSE OF THE WAY YOU PERCEIVE, OR THINK ABOUT YOUR ENVIRONMENT.

I inferred something in that last paragraph that is so fundamental to my THINK & GROW BALLS philosophy that I'm going to mention it again, except this time directly:

YOU CAN CONTROL THE WAY YOU FEEL AND YOU CAN DO IT BY CONTROLLING YOUR THOUGHTS.

Put another way, if your perception of a threat causes a subconscious signal to be sent from your mind to engage your body to release adrenaline and other chemical compounds, or hormones and other neurotransmitters, then you can control the way you feel.

All you need to do is change your perception. And, you can do that by changing your thinking.

If you can change the way you think, you can change the way your body will react to your thoughts (i.e., regulating the levels of hormones and neurotransmitters in your body and mind); thus, changing the way you feel.

If you change the way you feel, you'll automatically change the way you'll act. And, when you act differently, you'll get feedback from your environment. This feedback will affect your thinking as you adjust and modify your new behavior and this will in turn change your thoughts until they become established in your subconscious mind. When these new thoughts become habit and your new attitude becomes automatic, I guarantee you, your life will change for the better.

In the next chapter, I'll teach you about the most important natural chemicals of the human body. These are the "feel-good" chemicals that give you the experience of your emotions, all of them. And, I'm going to show you how to use your mind to help regulate these chemicals so you can regulate how you feel.

But, before I can teach you how to regulate them, you must understand them and the roles they play on your body.

So, without further ado, it's time to THINK & GROW BALLS!

# Heat

"The problem with most people is that they think with their hopes or fears or wishes rather than their minds." – Walter Duranty

## The "Feel-Good" Chemicals of the Human Body

In this chapter, I want to teach you about a group of chemical compounds created naturally in your brain and body. This group of chemicals are what I like to call, "The Feel-Good" (TFG) chemicals. I call them "feel-good" because they are chemicals produced in the body with only one purpose, to regulate how we feel, good OR bad (I like being optimistic).

There are two types of chemical compounds that make up TFG chemicals: hormones and neurotransmitters. Both of these chemical groups have a single purpose in the body yet they each carry out their tasks differently.

Hormones are chemical messengers that carry signals from one cell or group of cells to another via the blood. (Body)

Neurotransmitters are chemical messengers that are used to relay, amplify, and modulate signals between a neuron and another cell. (Brain)

There are many chemicals in each of these groups; however, I'm only going to focus on the most important ones. What's important to remember as I go over each of these TFGs is that these are BOTH hormones and neurotransmitters, giving you an indication of just how important they are to how you perceive, interpret, decide, and respond to your environment.

Epinephrine (AKA adrenaline) – Epinephrine is a "fight-or-flight" hormone that plays a central role in the short-term stress reaction. It is released from the adrenal glands when danger threatens or in an emergency. Such triggers may be threatening, exciting, or environmental stressor conditions such as high noise levels or bright light.

When secreted into the bloodstream, it rapidly prepares the body for action in emergency situations. The hormone boosts the supply of oxygen and glucose to the brain and muscles, while suppressing other non-emergency bodily processes (digestion in particular).

Adverse reactions to epinephrine include palpitations, tachycardia (elevated heart beat), anxiety, headache, tremor, hypertension (tightness of the muscles), and acute pulmonary edema.

Epinephrine synthesis is solely under the control of the central nervous system and via the sympathetic nervous system triggers the release of epinephrine into the bloodstream from the adrenal gland in the body.

Norepinephrine (AKA noradrenaline) – Along with epinephrine, norepinephrine underlies the "fight-or-flight" response, directly increasing heart rate, triggering the release of glucose from energy stores, and increasing skeletal muscle readiness.

It is released from the adrenal medulla of the adrenal glands as a hormone into the blood, but it is also a neurotransmitter in the central nervous system and sympathetic nervous system where it is released from noradrenergic neurons during synaptic transmission.

Norepinephrin is released when a host of physiological changes are activated by a stressful event.

Norepinephrin is naturally released both in the central nervous system where it helps control alertness and arousal, and from peripheral sympathetic nerves where it exerts diverse effects on its target organs.  It has come to be recognized as playing a large role in attention and focus.

Dopamine – Dopamine is a hormone and neurotransmitter occurring in a wide variety of animals, including both vertebrates and invertebrates.  It is a precursor to norepinephrin (noradrenaline) and then epinephrine (adrenaline) in the biosynthetic pathways for these neurotransmitters.

Dopamine has many functions in the brain, including important roles in behavior and cognition, motor activity, motivation and reward, regulation of milk production, sleep, mood, attention, and learning.

The phasic responses of dopamine neurons are observed when an unexpected reward is presented.  THESE RESPONSES TRANSFER THE ONSET OF A CONDITIONED STIMULUS AFTER REPEATED PAIRINGS WITH THE REWARD.  Further, dopamine neurons are depressed when the expected reward is omitted.  Thus, dopamine neurons seem to encode the prediction error of rewarding outcomes.  In nature, we learn to repeat behaviors that lead to maximum rewards.  DOPAMINE IS THEREFORE BELIEVED BY MANY TO PROVIDE A TEACHING SIGNAL TO PARTS OF THE BRAIN RESPONSIBLE FOR ACQUIRING NEW BEHAVIOR.

Dopamine is commonly associated with the pleasure system of the brain, providing feelings of enjoyment and reinforcement to motivate a person proactively to perform certain activities.  Dopamine is released by naturally rewarding experiences such as food, sex, the use of certain drugs, and NEUTRAL STIMULI THAT BECOME ASSOCIATED WITH THEM.

Read that whole last paragraph again.  The last part is extremely important to my theory.

It has been argued that dopamine is more associated with anticipatory desire and motivation (commonly referred to as "wanting") as opposed to actual consummatory pleasure (commonly referred to as "liking").

Sociability is also closely tied to dopamine neurotransmission and it may also have a role in the salience (notability) of perceived objects and events, with potentially important stimuli such as: 1) rewarding things, or 2) dangerous or threatening things seeming more noticeable or important.

Endorphins – Produced in both the body and brain in vertebrates, they endorphins resemble opiates in their abilities to produce analgesia and a sense of well-being.  In other words, they work as "natural pain killers".

The name "endorphin" is an abbreviation of "endogenous morphine", which literally means, "morphine produced naturally in the body".

The term "endorphin rush" has been adopted in popular speech to refer to feelings of exhilaration brought on by pain, danger, or other forms of stress.

Another widely publicized effect of endorphin production is the so-called "runner's high", which is said to occur when strenuous exercise takes a person over a threshold that activates endorphin production.  Endorphins are released during long, continuous workouts, when the level of intensity is between moderate and high, and breathing is difficult.  This also corresponds with the time the muscles use up their stored glycogen and begin functioning with only oxygen.  Workouts that are most likely to produce endorphins include running, swimming, cross-country skiing, long distance rowing, bicycling, weight lifting, aerobics, or playing a sport such as basketball, soccer, or football.

There is some current debate about just how significant a role endorphins play in the "runner's high" and that the high comes from completing a challenge rather than as a result of exertion.  Recent studies show that the effect may also be attributed to another chemical naturally produced in the brain and body, a chemical called anandamide.

Anandamide – a cannabinoid neurotransmitter found in animal and human organs, especially the brain.  Directly related to the primary psychoactive cannabinoid found in cannabis, THC, anandamidc is important in the regulation of feeding behavior and the neural generation of motivation and pleasure.  Both anandamide and THC enhance food intake in animals and humans, an effect that is sometimes called the "marijuana munchies".  Anandamide has been shown to be involved in working memory and studies are underway to explore what role it plays in human behavior, such as eating and sleep patterns and pain relief.

Serotonin – a neurotransmitter in the central nervous system and the gastrointestinal tract of animals, including humans.  Serotonin is also found in many mushroom and plants, including fruits and vegetables.

In the central nervous system, serotonin is believed to play an important role in the regulation of anger, aggression, body temperature, mood, sleep, vomiting, sexuality, and appetite.

Low levels of serotonin may be associated with several disorders, namely increase in aggressive and angry behaviors, clinical depression, obsessive-compulsive disorder (OCD), migraine, irritable bowel syndrome, tinnitus, fibromyalgia, bipolar disorder, and anxiety disorders.  If neurons of the brainstem that make serotonin are abnormal in infants, there is a risk of sudden infant death syndrome (SIDS).  And, low levels of serotonin may also be associated with intense religious experiences.

Serotonin taken orally does not pass into the pathways of the central nervous system because it does not cross the blood-brain barrier. However, tryptophan and its metabolite 5-hydroxytryptophan (5-HTP), from which serotonin is synthesized, can and do cross the blood-brain barrier. THESE AGENTS ARE AVAILABLE AS DIETARY SUPPLEMENTS AND MAY BE EFFECTIVE SEROTONERGIC AGENTS.

It should also be noted that tryptophan is also in a lot of meats (e.g., turkey), that when you eat in large amounts (i.e., holidays), makes you sleepy. Studies now show that your brain is synthesizing serotonin from these precursors that results in your feeling warm, relaxed, content, and tired (snooze). It's also probably the reason you want to take a nap at work right after lunch.

I've just talked about six chemical compounds that your body naturally produces to modulate how you feel. I believe that as modern medicine and psychology progress society will learn about others, but for now, these six neurotransmitters and hormones are the major factors and key players in making you feel one way or another.

As you go about your day, take note of how you are feeling. Find it's corresponding emotion and gauge the levels of these chemical compounds running through your brain and body. Of course you will never be able to actually quantify the amounts and that's okay... that's not important. What is important is that you establish a baseline reading. Once you have a baseline, you can then work on raising or decreasing the levels affecting you.

By now, many of you are asking, "but, if I concentrate on my emotions and the chemicals causing them, aren't I using my conscious mind to control it? What's with all the subconscious stuff?"

The answer to that question is that it may seem as if your conscious mind is controlling your feelings, but the chemical compounds in your body are controlled by your sympathetic nervous system that is actually controlled by your subconscious. You must "reprogram" or "condition" your subconscious mind to hand partial control of your sympathetic nervous system reaction to your conscious mind. Ultimately, you will be able to control your emotions and feelings at will, regardless of the level of fear you experience or your response to it.

In the next chapter, I'm going to teach you how your conscious mind can communicate with your subconscious mind. These are all techniques that have proven to blur the boundary between these two parts of the mind so the conscious mind can imprint beneficial thoughts on the subconscious.

You with me so far? Good. You're getting closer on how to THINK & GROW BALLS!

# Ignition

"There is nothing either good or bad, but thinking makes it so." –
William Shakespeare

## Techniques for Changing Your Thinking Habits

In this chapter, I'm going to give you the tools you're going to need to reprogram your subconscious mind with courageous thoughts. I'm going to teach you techniques on how to use your conscious mind to communicate and imprint thoughts in your subconscious mind. There are no miracles here. Each one of these techniques is clinically proven to help, some by themselves alone and others in combination with each other. In no particular order, here they are: (the following is from Wikipedia.org)

Autosuggestion – a term used for positive or negative physical symptoms explained by the thoughts and beliefs of a person. For example, some will experience more pain when they think it will hurt. Headaches sometimes go away after taking a painkiller, but before the painkiller could actually start acting on its own. Related to this is the placebo-effect (a clinical term used to classify subjects in a study who experience the expected effect(s) or result(s) even though they were given a sugar pill, evidence of mind-over-matter).

This influence of the mind on the body can be used in a positive way to improve the way a person feels (mentally and physically).

Autosuggestion is a process by which an individual trains the subconscious mind to believe something, or systematically schematizes the person's own mental associations, usually for a given purpose. This is accomplished through self-hypnosis methods or repetitive, constant self-affirmations, and may be seen as a form of self-induced brainwashing. The acceptance of autosuggestion may be quickened through mental visualization of that which the individual would like to believe. Its success is typically correlated with the consistency of its use and the length of time over which it is used (practice makes perfect). Autosuggestion can be seen as an aspect of prayer, self-exhorting "pep talks", meditation, and other activities.

Autosuggestion is most commonly accomplished by presenting (either though caressing or bombarding) one's mind with repetitive thoughts (negative or positive), until those thoughts become internalized. Practitioners typically hope to transmute thoughts into beliefs, and even into actualities. Visualizing the manifestations of a belief, verbally affirming it, and thinking it using one's "internal voice", are typical means of influencing one's mind via repetitive autosuggestion.

APPLICATIONS OF DELIBERATE AUTOSUGGESTION ARE INTENDED TO CHANGE: THE WAY ONE BELIEVES, PERCEIVES, OR THINKS; ONE'S ACTS; OR THE WAY ONE IS COMPOSED PHYSICALLY OR PHYSIOLOGICALLY. An example might be individuals reading nightly aloud a statement they have written describing how they would like to be, then repeating the statement in their mind until they fall asleep. PEOPLE HAVE ATTRIBUTED CHANGES TO SUCH A NIGHTLY ROUTINE OR SIMILAR EMPLOYMENT OF AUTOSUGGESTION, FOR EXAMPLE, INCREASED CONFIDENCE, THE CONQUERING OF LIFE-LONG FEARS, HEIGHTENED MENTAL FACULTIES (E.G., ABILITY TO CALCULATE MATHEMATICS OR READ AT A QUICKER RATE), ERADICATION OF DISEASES OR INFECTIONS FROM ONE'S BODY, AND EVEN IMPROVED EYESIGHT AND GROWING TALLER.

The same type of effect that deliberate autosuggestion may achieve can also be seen in individuals <u>NOT</u> consciously trying to program themselves through autosuggestion. <u>The dominant thoughts that occupy a person's conscious mind, if constantly present over an extended period of time, may have the effect</u>

of training that person's subconscious mind to organize that individual's beliefs according to those thoughts. In this sense, the mechanisms of pathological fixations (bad habits) and obsessions to some extent resemble the process of autosuggestion.

Autosuggestion is differentiated from brainwashing in that the suggestions given during the sessions originate with the individual, rather than originating with suggestions from others.

Johannes Schultz developed this theory as Autogenic Training.

Autogenic Training – a relaxation technique developed by the German psychiatrist Johannes Schultz and first published in 1932. The technique involves the daily practice of sessions that last around 15 minutes, usually in the morning, at lunchtime, and in the evening. During each session, the practitioner will repeat a set of visualizations that induce a state of relaxation. Each session can be practiced in a position chosen amongst a set of recommended postures (e.g., lying down, sitting meditation, sitting like a rag doll, etc.) The technique can be used to alleviate many stress-induced psychosomatic behaviors.

Schultz emphasized parallels to techniques in yoga and meditation. It is a method for influencing one's autonomic nervous system.

Autogenic Training restores the balance between the activity of the sympathetic (fight-or-flight) and the parasympathetic (rest and digest) branches of the autonomic nervous system. This has important health benefits, as the parasympathetic activity promotes digestion and bowel movements, lowers the blood pressure, slows the heart rate, and promotes the functions of the immune system.

Autogenic Training can be adapted to a series of conditions including: heart problems such as myocardial infarction, diabetes, psychotic conditions such as schizophrenia, glaucoma, alcohol or drug abuse, and epilepsy.

For a great introduction into Autogenic Training, visit the following website:

http://www.guidetopsychology.com/autogen.htm

Affirmation – the declaration that something is true or a positive value judgment.

An affirmation is a form of autosuggestion in which a statement of a desirable intention or condition of the world or mind is deliberately meditated on and/or repeated in order to implant it in the subconscious mind. Many believers recommend accompanying recitations with mental visualization of a desired outcome.

Affirmation can be viewed positively as a mobilization of one's inner resources. For example, believers would consider "I AM making more room in my life for success every day" a much wiser affirmation than "I WILL win the lottery today!"

Affirmations are always phrased in the first person and usually in a present tense ("I AM") rather than a future tense ("I WILL") in order to increase the realization of the statement for the affirmation. Affirmations are believed to be a very powerful means of reprogramming the subconscious mind. They appear to be most effective when repeated in a quiet and restful state of mind and body, and when the desired outcome is vividly experienced in one's mind and resulting emotions are felt.

Desensitization – a process for mitigating the harmful effects of phobias or other disorders. It also occurs when an emotional response is repeatedly evoked in situations in which the action tendency that is associated with the emotion proves irrelevant or unnecessary.

Desensitization is one of my favorite methods for reducing my fear and anxiety of specific situations. I have used this method so many times in my life that it has become part of my personality. I strongly recommend this technique as it involves ACTION and staring fear directly in the face, but on your terms. For example, if you are afraid of talking to people of the opposite sex, go to an environment where you are comfortable (small coffee shops, pubs, stores) and talk to every person you see, regardless of their gender. If you are afraid of arguing and confrontation, join a debate class or a self-defense program. If you're afraid of spiders, print out a huge color picture of the scariest and most deadly spider you can find on the Internet, frame it, and hang it in a place where you'll see it all the time. You'll find that by overexposing yourself to your feared situations results in you eventually becoming "numb" to them. And many times, you are afraid of or become anxious about things you do not understand, so desensitization can also be done by doing research and studying the things that you fear.

The above techniques are all from the traditional school of psychology, and involve classical conditioning where you change your programmed response to particular stimuli. There are many more techniques for dealing with fear, anxiety, and trauma that you may want to explore if this material interests you.

There is another school of psychology that uses an interpersonal communication model that is based on the subjective study of language, communication, and personal change that has grown in popularity over the last 40 years. This alternative approach to psychology is called Neuro-Linguistic Programming, or NLP for short.

NLP was co-created by Richard Bandler and linguist John Grinder in the 1970s with the aim of discovering what made certain individuals more successful than their peers.

Perhaps most generally, NLP aims to increase behavioral flexibility (i.e., choice) by the manipulation of subjective experience, either by practitioner/trainer or by self-application). Some of the main ideas include:

- The way an individual thinks about a problem or desired outcome has an effect on the way he or she will deal with problems and choose a certain course of action.

- When communicating with someone, rather than just listening to and responding to what a person is saying, NLP aims to also respond to the structure of verbal communication and non-verbal cues.

- The NLP Meta model questioning is intended to clarify what has been left out or distorted in communication.

- The NLP Milton model uses non-specific and metaphoric language allowing the listener to fill in the gaps, making their own meaning from what is being said, finding their own solutions and inner resources, challenging and reframing irrational beliefs.

- The actual state someone is in when setting a goal or choosing a course of action is also considered important. A number of techniques in NLP aim to enhance states by anchoring resourceful states associated with personal experience or model states by imitating others.

The founders of NLP emphasize that in their experience, experts in human communication all have a similar approach, and IT IS THIS APPROACH (AND NOT THE TECHNICAL SKILLS) WHICH DISTINGUISHES THEM, AND WHICH CAN BE LEARNED.

Analyzing further, Grinder and Bandler stated that there were a very few common traits such people – whether top therapists, top executives, or top salespeople – all seemed to share:

1. Everything they did in their work, was pro-active (rather than reactive), directed moment to moment by well-formed outcomes rather than formalized fixed beliefs.

2. They were exceedingly flexible in approach and refused to be tied down to using their skills in any one fixed way of thinking or working.

3. They were extremely aware moment by moment, of the non-verbal feedback they were getting, and responded to it – usually in kind rather than by analyzing it.

4. They enjoyed the challenges of difficult [people], seeing them as a chance to learn rather than an intractable problem.

5. They respected [people] as someone doing the best they knew how (rather than judging them negatively).

6. They had certain common skills and things they were aware of and noticed, intuitively "wired in".

7. They kept trying many different things until they learned enough about the structure holding a problem in place to change it.

They (Grinder and Bandler) summarized their findings:

"You need only three things to be an absolutely exquisite communicator. We have found that there are three major patterns in the behavior of every therapeutic wizard we've talked to – and executives, and salespeople. The first one is to know what outcome you want. The second is that you need flexibility in your behavior. You need to be able to generate lots and lots of different behaviors to find out what responses you get.  The thirds is you need to have enough sensory experience to notice when you get the responses you want…"

The basic principles and presuppositions of NLP are:

- The map is not the territory.

- Life and mind are systematic processes

- Behind every behavior there is a positive intention.

- There is no failurc, only feedback.

- The meaning of the communication is the response it produces, not the intended communication.

- One cannot not communicate.

- Choice is better than no choice.

- People already have all the internal resources they need to succeed.

- Multiple descriptions are better than one.


There are two powerful techniques used in NLP to help reprogram the way you think and the effect that thinking has on your body and feelings.  They are described below as follows:

Anchoring – the process by which memory recall, state change, or other responses become associated with (anchored to) some stimulus, in such a way that perception of the stimulus (the anchor) leads by reflex to the anchored response occurring. The stimulus may be quite neutral or even out of conscious awareness, and the response may be either positive or negative.  They are capable of being formed and reinforced by repeated stimuli, and thus are analogous to classical conditioning.

Basic anchoring involves in essence, the elicitation of a strong congruent experience of a desired state, whilst using some notable stimulus (touch, word, sight) at the time this is most fully realized. In many cases, repetition of the stimulus will associate and restore the experience of the state.

There are refinements and sophistications in setting anchors this way, and subtleties involved in order to both set them with precision, and to avoid accidentally neutralizing them in the process of setting them up.

Anchors can come in many possible forms; verbal phrases, physical touches or sensations, certain sights and sounds, or internally, such as words one says to oneself, or memories and states one is in. An expansive view is that almost everything one perceives acts as an anchor, in the sense that perceiving it tends to trigger reflexively some thought or feeling or response.

Anchoring is a natural process that usually occurs without our awareness, and may have positive impact, or be maladaptive. For example, a voice tonality that resembles the characteristics of one's perception of an "angry voice" may not actually be the result of anger, but will usually trigger an emotional response in the person perceiving the tonality to have the traits of anger.

There are certain speculations as to what criteria must be met before an anchor can be properly formed. Most agree that the trigger must be:

- Specific – otherwise the subject will not begin to sensitize to it.

- Intermittent – if it were constant then desensitization would eventually occur.

- Unique, specific, and prompt – otherwise the anchor will fail to elicit and reinforce any one single response due to many different reactions being associated to the trigger.

Here are some examples of anchors that trigger specific responses:

- If, when young, you participated in family activities that gave you great pleasure, the pleasure was associated with the activity itself, so when you think of the activity or are reminded of it you tend to experience some pleasurable feeling.

- Looking through an old family photo album stirs pleasant memories and some of the feelings associated with them.

- A child's comforter in an unfamiliar situation.

- An old love song awakens a romantic mood.

- The smell of freshly baked apple pies brings back memories of a happy, carefree childhood.

- Revisiting an old school or a place with powerful memories.

Anchoring is a process that goes on around and within us all the time, whether we are aware of it or not. Most of the time we are not consciously aware of why we feel as we do – indeed we may not realize we have responded in some cases, which makes anchoring a much more powerful force in our lives.

Anchoring is used in NLP to facilitate state management. In this sense an anchor is set up to be triggered by a consciously chosen stimulus, deliberately linked by practice to a known useful state, to provide reflexive access to that state at will. This may be used for exam nerves, overcoming fear, feelings such as happiness or determination, or to recollect how one will feel if a good resolution is kept.

Reframing – a technique used to describe changing the context or representation of a problem. More precisely, one of the most effective techniques for achieving almost any desired change in NLP is the Six-Step Reframe. Another effective method is the Context Reframe.

Reframing occurs in life regardless of NLP, and is a common means by which meanings get created and lost in various situations, either deliberately or by happenstance.

Anthony Robbins, a best-selling author, motivational speaker, and practitioner of NLP wrote, "A signal has meaning only in the frame or context in which we perceive it." For example, if a person is resting in bed and hears his bedroom door open, that exact same noise will have two totally different meanings to him and evoke drastically different reactions depending on whether (1) he is alone in a locked house, or (2) he had previously invited his friend over and left the back door to his house unlocked. According to Anthony Robins,

> "If we perceive something as a liability, that's the message we deliver to our brain. Then the brain produces states that make it a reality. If we change our frame of reference by looking at the same situation from a different point of view, we can change the way we respond in life. We can change our representation or perception about anything and in a moment change our states and behaviors. This is what reframing is all about."

For example, say a college student breaks his leg during summer vacation. He is crestfallen, because he can no longer play tennis and golf with his family and friends. A few days later, he realizes that he now has the quiet, alone time to learn how to play the guitar, something he had always wanted to do but had been too busy to attempt. He then discovers he has great aptitude for music and becomes a decent guitar player by summer's end.  One year later, he changes his major to music. After graduation he embarks on a successful music career. Years later, his friends recall how unfortunate his leg break was that summer, and he says, "Breaking my leg was the best thing that ever happened to me!"  From then on, whenever he is disabled by injury or illness, he recalls the lesson and is far less despondent over his temporary disability than he otherwise would have been, as he takes the opportunity to do something novel.

The Six-Step Reframe is used to replace an unwanted behavior or bad habit with a more desirable one – while keeping the benefits, or secondary gain, of the old behavior.

NLP presupposes that "every behavior has a positive intention," and that any undesirable behavior a person has will also have a positive benefit behind it (often subconsciously).

## The Six-Step Reframe

The Six-Step Reframe uses a mild trance state, negotiation, and creativity from subconscious resources to change the "part" that's causing the behavior.

1. Identify the behavior to change.

2. Set up signals with the part causing the behavior.

3. Identify the positive intention behind the behavior.

4. Generate a number of possible alternative behaviors that will equally satisfy the same intent.

5. Choose the favored three replacement behaviors.

6. Check to see if there is any other internal conflict regarding the change.

## Context Reframing

The meaning of any behavior or event exists only in relationship to the context in which it occurs.

Every behavior is appropriate in some context. With a context reframe, a person takes the disliked behavior and asks, "Where could this behavior be useful?" or "In what other context would this particular behavior be of value?"

A context reframe leaves the meaning of a behavior the same and shows how it could be a useful response in a different context.

NLP is a fascinating and powerful method for changing the way you think in order to change the way you respond to specific situations. If this topic interests you, I recommend you read *Frogs into Princes*, by the founders of NLP, Bandler and Grinder and *Unlimited Power*, by Anthony Robbins.

There is another technique that I use that I like to call the "So What?" technique. It is a very easy technique to start implementing in your life right away. It goes like this. The next time you start to feel fear, anxiety, or panic and your fight-or-flight response kicks in and the feel good chemicals of your brain and body start to circulate through your system, just stop and take a few deep breaths. While doing this, visualize in your mind the WORST POSSIBLE OUTCOME of the situation you're facing. Then, make the decision TO BE OKAY WITH IT. This works because when you let your imagination run wild with your fear, you will often times think up scenarios that AREN'T VERY LIKELY. In other words, there's a very slim chance that what you fear might happen actually will. Using this technique, you direct your imagination to a specific worst-case scenario (preventing your imagination from running wild), and then you make a conscious decision to be okay with the outcome even if it does happen; you say, "so what?" to yourself. If you do this often enough, reason will kick in and tell you that DEATH IS ALWAYS THE WORST-CASE SCENARIO, but to quote Napoleon Hill, "What is death but a long, peaceful sleep? And, I like sleep." And, you will find yourself not fearing many situations.

Self-Hypnosis & Meditation

As a conclusion to this chapter, I wanted to talk briefly about hypnosis and meditation. There are many terms that describe the act of "being in a trance" or "quieting your mind" or "becoming one with your body" or "centering yourself" but these two terms reflect both Eastern and Western philosophy so I'll use them. For the purpose of this e-book, I'll use the term hypnosis to encompass both philosophies.

Not surprisingly, hypnosis is still considered a pseudo-science by mainstream society. I understand this because hypnosis is a very personal experience and one that not all people can experience in the same way, if at all.

Each technique I have described above is designed to work best when the mind is in a "trance-like" state. Many practitioners of these techniques use hypnosis as a way to induce a trance-like state so classical conditioning and NLP reprogramming can imprint itself on the subconscious mind more efficiently.

Self-hypnosis is no different that hypnosis except that you perform it on yourself. Regardless of whether you believe in hypnosis or not, the techniques in this chapter will work better if you can quiet your conscious mind and relax your body. I know of a technique that will accomplish this without infringing on any of your beliefs and I suggest that you use it to practice the techniques in this chapter.

(I recommend you read *Dynamic Thinking* and *A Practical Guide to Self-Hypnosis*, both by Melvin Powers to better help you understand how to communicate with your subconscious mind.)

The technique works like this.

In the last few moments of consciousness before you fall asleep and in the last few moments of sleep before you awake exists a period of time in which your conscious mind and subconscious mind communicate directly with each other.

[Have you ever had the conscious thought that you were in a dream or had a dream that you thought was real?  These thoughts and dreams only occur during this "crossover" phase of your conscious and subconscious minds.  It is the first phase of sleep (or the last phase of consciousness, depending on how you look at it).]

In this crossover phase, your body is in a state of extreme rest, your conscious mind activity is so slow it hands the reigns of control to your subconscious mind to record and categorize the day's experiences and calculations and/or prepare for the upcoming day's events.

DURING THIS PHASE, USE THE CLASSICAL CONDITIONING AND NLP TECHNIQUES TO IMPRINT WHATEVER THOUGHTS YOU WANT ON YOUR SUBCONSCIOUS MIND.

(Another method to practice conscious control over your subconscious mind is to try to lower or speed up your heart rate.  I like this method because it gives me immediate feedback as to whether or not it's working and I can use it virtually anywhere.  The method is very simple.  Try calming your mind while focusing on your heartbeat.  You don't need to check your pulse (but you can if you're on an exercise machine of some sort) or be accurate.  Just notice how fast it is.  Now take deep breaths.  In through the nose... chest out and shoulders back... chin raised.  Now out through the mouth. Use your diaphragm to power your breathing.  Not your chest.  When you breathe you should notice your stomach moving in and out... not your chest.  Focus on your breathing.  Focus on your heartbeat. Now, say the following words to yourself, "SLOW, CALM, OK, DOWN, RELAX".  Repeat them.  Mix up the order of them.  Only say one for a while.  Shuffle them.  In moments, you will notice your heartbeat has slowed... your muscles are relaxed... you feel oxygenated... your mind is clear.  When you feel comfortable with slowing your heartbeat, try speeding it up.  Reverse everything.  YOU ARE IN CONTROL!  You are DOING mind over matter!)

This may come easy for you or it might take some practice.  Either way, with practice it will become easier.  Eventually, you will be able to prolong this crossover phase so you will be able to imprint whatever you want for as long as you want.  But, that is a topic for an e-book all by itself.

For now, just start with one technique and one thought or message.  When you have that one imprinted, move on to another.  The idea is to make this a part of your morning and evening routine (and nap time, if you take them) so that this dialogue between your conscious and subconscious mind become habitual.  Mastery of this technique can require years of practice, so be patient and just believe that it will work.

Or, maybe you DO believe in hypnosis and you want to enlist the help of a professional.  If you do, that's great!  But, if you do this yourself, you'll get the advantage of having your own internal voice imprint your thoughts and you'll save some cash.

* Please note that these techniques DO work (for good and for bad) and they can be very powerful, even if you do them yourself.  Some people may have legitimate mental health disorders that require the attention of a trained and certified professional.  In suggesting these techniques, I assume you to be of "normal" mental health.  IF YOU ARE UNSURE, PLEASE SEEK PROFESSIONAL ADVICE BEFORE ATTEMPTING THESE TECHNIQUES.

Now, you have all the pieces you need to reduce your fear and enlarge your courage.  It's time for the fun stuff!  In the next chapter, I'm going to teach you how to combine all that you have learned into a working philosophy that can help you live decisively.  It's time to THINK & GROW BALLS!

# Liftoff

"I must not fear.  Fear is the mind-killer.  Fear is the little death that brings total obliteration.  I will face my fear.  I will permit it to pass over me and through me.  And when it has gone past I will turn the inner eye to see its path.  Where the fear has gone there will be nothing.  Only I will remain." – Frank Herbert

## Thrust, Gaining Momentum, & Developing Inertia

As an introduction to this chapter, I want to talk about two well-known celebrities in America that emulate my THINK & GROW BALLS! Philosophy ideally.  These two figures are Tiger Woods and Criss Angel.  One is an athlete, the other is an illusionist, but I believe they both have mastered the ability to control their thoughts and their feelings to control the chemicals flowing through their body so that they can "perform under pressure".

Let's take Tiger Woods to start.  Clearly, he is one of the best golfers to ever swing a club.  In several years, he may prove himself to be THE best ever.  EVERYONE who has watched his career over the last ten years has asked the question, "How does he remain so calm under pressure?"  Tiger has been in some extremely grueling sudden death playoffs and has won most of them.  He has comeback from behind on the last day of a tournament to win so many times I have lost count.  His competitors FEAR him.  None of them want to be paired with him on the final day of a tournament... EVER!

What mystical power does Tiger Woods have that his competitors don't?  What is his competitive edge?  Why do spectators stare and gasp at him in awe while those competing against him crumble in his presence?  How does he keep complete composure when other men crack?

I'd like to read you a passage from a book entitled, *Fearless Golf: Conquering the Mental Game* by Dr. Gio Valiante.  This passage clearly defines what sets champions apart from everyone else. It also suggests why Tiger Woods is so damn good:

> When I turn my critical eye on all these great moments, there is one thing the great champions manage to overcome. It is a greater foe than any apparently invincible opponent, than any brutally penal golf course itself or even the unshakable enormity of any once-in-a-lifetime moment. It is fear, the most critical impediment to playing golf to your greatest potential. It matters not if you are a weekend hacker in the later stages of your usual Saturday game or a PGA Tour champion stepping to the eighteenth tee with a one-shot lead. If there is one universal truth to golfers of all levels, it is fear, fear of failure, fear of embarrassment, fear of the unexpected, fear of poor judgment. It is fear of long courses, of short courses, of narrow courses, of hilly courses and flat courses. It is fear of water hazards and sand bunkers, of short putts and long putts. We even fear things that in reality aren't there, like that flagstick that looks to be inches beyond a bunker when it's really a dozen or more yards.
>
> It is fear of playing with certain people or against certain people or even in front of certain people. It is even fear of knowing we are afraid, and it gnaws on our consciousness, undermines our skills, sabotages our capabilities, and infects our confidence.

I don't know the man, but in my opinion Tiger Woods has mastered the ability to control his thoughts. In turn he can control his feelings and emotions. By doing this, he is a virtual puppet master of the chemicals running through his body. Whether Tiger knows this himself or not, I can't say... but I believe he can do this AT WILL.

HE HAS MASTERED FEAR.

HE IS THE MASTER OF HIS OWN DOMAIN.

Oh, heart racing a bit too much... I'll just slow it down... done.

Oh, palms are too sweaty... I'll relax and make them stop... done.

Oh, shaking too much... I'll center myself... done.

Oh, forgot to cash my last check... I'll focus on the present... done.

I believe he has obtained this ability to control his mind and body through HARDCORE CLASSICAL CONDITIONING and NEURO-LINGUISTIC PROGRAMMING.  I believe his father taught him how to do it.  And, I think his power is a gift.

I think Tiger Woods has BALLS.

But, guess what?

He is still human... and that means WE ALL CAN LEARN THIS POWER!

Think what you can do if you had this power.  The ability to keep your composure at all times... when others are melting away, you are strong and steadfast... you're not going anywhere.

Would your life be different?

What could you do now if you had the power to be your own puppet master?

How would your future look if you knew you would keep your composure through thick and thin?

What would you become if you mastered fear and its effect on your body?

What if you could think clearly in times of extreme stress so that you had a better chance of making the right decisions?

What if you could be decisive in your life?

Would you use your power for good?

Would you become a positive leader?

Would you get that car?  That job?  That love interest?  That house?  That wardrobe?  That bank account?

Would you take that long-awaited vacation?

Would you start that business?

Would you dust off the home-gym equipment and do a few sets?

Would you set some high goals for yourself?

How will you know when you've achieved them?

How will you celebrate?

What would be different about you?

Where would you live?

What hobbies or activities would you involve yourself in?

Who would your friends be?

Would you teach others how to get "balls" or would you keep the power and awe for yourself?

Would you stand up for yourself and the ones you love?

Would you have a cause?

Who or what would you help?

Would you finally donate money to charity... now that you have plenty of it?

Think about what living a life with BALLS will mean to you!

Would you live decisively?

Would you make a statement about yourself?

What legacy will you leave behind?

How will the world know you even existed?

What will you do to prove that YOU ARE GOOD ENOUGH?


Hopefully, with those questions I got your mind racing with answers.


Now, let's talk about Criss Angel. He's probably not as well known as Tiger Woods, but he's just as interesting and entertaining. Now, for me, the jury is still out on the complete believability of his illusions. But, what I am convinced of is his ability to control pain. Recently, he visited with a child who has a medical condition that requires frequent injections with needles. The boy finds this experience to be extremely painful so he asked Criss how he overcomes physical pain in his performances. Criss replied that he focuses his thoughts on the pain so intensely that eventually he becomes "numb" to the pain.

I find Criss' answer to be fascinating.

Could it be that he has somehow discovered a way to use his thoughts to trigger the production and release of endorphins or other natural painkillers in his body? Is he using his CONSCIOUS MIND TO CONTROL HIS SUBCONSCIOUS MIND IN THE PRESENT? I firmly believe that he has.

He has mastered "mind over matter".

I believe he has obtained this ability through HARDCORE CLASSICAL CONDITIONING and NEURO-LINGUISTIC PROGRAMMING.

He is a master of overcoming pain.

But, before he could master pain, he had to master fear first.  After all, he deliberately puts himself in situations that WILL DEFINITELY INFLICT PAIN.  In order to do that, he had to overcome his FEAR OF PAIN.

He believes he has this ability to master fear and pain.

He KNOWS he has this ability.

He's done it time and time again.

He has BALLS!

And, guess what?

Yep, you guessed it.  He's human, too.  And, you can acquire this ability to.

WHAT WOULD YOU DO WITH A FRACTION OF THESE ABILITIES?

You can master fear.

You can have BALLS!

All you have to do is THINK & GROW BALLS!


So, what do you have to do?  How can you start down the path of shrinking your fear and enlarging your courage?  Well, I'm going to share with you the secret on how to do it.  But, here's the catch... I can't do it for you.

YOU HAVE TO MAKE THE COMMITMENT TO YOURSELF TO LIVE DECISIVELY!

MAKE A COMMITMENT TO LIVE A LIFE WITH BALLS SO YOU CAN ACHIEVE ANYTHING YOU SET YOUR MIND TO!

If you don't make this commitment, my philosophy will never work for you. This process takes mastery... and mastery takes practice and time.

IN FACT, IF YOU WON'T MAKE THIS COMMITMENT TO YOURSELF, STOP READING THIS E-BOOK RIGHT NOW, SEND ME AN E-MAIL SAYING "I DON'T BELIEVE THIS WILL WORK FOR ME" AND I WILL PROMPTLY REFUND YOUR MONEY. <u>THE REST OF THIS E-BOOK FROM THIS POINT ON (.) IS FOR BELIEVERS ONLY!</u>

## Achieving Escape Velocity

Before I introduce you to Escape Velocity, I want to talk about something EXTREMELY important. IN ORDER FOR THIS E-BOOK AND THE HARD-EARNED MONEY YOU SPENT TO OBTAIN YOUR COPY TO BE USEFUL, YOU MUST KNOW YOUR PURPOSE... YOU MUST HAVE YOUR GOAL IN MIND... YOUR DESTINATION... YOUR MISSION. You must know specifically what you want. This e-book is meant to help you get the thrust you need to take your first steps towards obtaining your mission. No book on the planet Earth can tell you what you really want to accomplish during your life. You must choose your own purpose. This is your Free Will.

You can do or be anything you want... but, you must know what "it" is before you can start your journey towards it. Otherwise, you are a boat adrift at sea with no sails and no rudder... a heat-seeking missile without a target. You will have nothing to guide you toward your destination.

(Whether you believe in fate or destiny or whatever you want to call it, doesn't matter. You'll fulfill your destiny or fate a lot faster if you know where you're headed.)

So, before I go any further launching you to the stars, I want to make sure you know what you want. Which star do you want to go to? And, I want you to be sure of it. Know it. Believe you can do it.

If you don't know what or where you want to go, please read *Think & Grow Rich: The 21st-Century Edition*. One of the main reasons why this book has been so successful is because it can cause an epiphany in your mind. This epiphany is discovering what your definite purpose is.

Once you read the book, reread this e-book. I'm trying to encourage you to take action towards your goal. I'm not trying to tell you what your goal is.

If you're still unsure what your purpose is, just ask your "internal" voice in the back of your mind. It is never wrong. Ask the question. It will tell you the answer.

Now, on to <u>Escape Velocity</u>…

In physics, escape velocity is the speed where the kinetic energy of an object is equal in magnitude to its potential energy in a gravitational field. It is commonly described as the speed needed to "break free" from a gravitational field.

In my philosophy, escape velocity is the amount of courage needed to break free from the gravitational field and the inertia of your previous decisions so you can launch and propel yourself towards your goal or definite purpose.

What do I mean by "gravitational field" and why is it something you need to "break free" of? Well, since you, at the present moment, are the total sum of all your decisions and experiences of your life so far, you've gathered a lot of momentum and inertia moving in your current direction.  If you want to grow balls and take action to change your life you're going to need a lot of energy to change your current course.  Much like shifting a locomotive into reverse at 85 miles per hour, the change in direction will not take place immediately.  Momentum and inertia must be overcome so that new energy can take over.  This momentum and inertia is the mental weight of your subconscious mind.  It's something you can't see, but it exists all around you... it orbits around you.  Your mental weight is caused by previously imprinted negative thoughts and affirmations throughout your life.  It's the habits that you have picked up over the years, both good and bad.  It is the energy that "holds you back" and "weighs you down".  It is "the Man" and all of societies expectations of you and their assumptions of you.  More important, mental weight is your perception of yourself and your perceived value to the world.  It is the Kryptonite necklace that you wear around your neck.  It's real.  It's powerful.  And, it doesn't have to be there.  You'll need to condition and reprogram your subconscious mind with positive thoughts and courageous affirmations until the positive thoughts get installed and overpower the playing field of your mind and tip the scales in your favor.  You can make certain decisions and do certain things to reduce this mental weight.  I'll talk more about this skill below.

I'm now going to tell you exactly what you need to do and in what order to achieve your own escape velocity.  There are eight steps in this process.... I call them "The Eight R's".  Not only do they describe how to shrink your fear and enlarge your courage, they describe how to prepare for the next time you'll need balls to get what you want.  Here they are in order:

1. Realize – You must realize that fear is an emotion and it plays an important and powerful role in the survival of our species (i.e., your survival).  Realize that fear manifests itself in your body in physical and predictable ways such as the engaging of the fight-or-flight response.  Realize what is happening to your mind and body when fear strikes.  Realize that chemical compounds being produced and released throughout your mind and body are making you feel afraid.  Realize how impaired

your decision-making abilities are. Realize that with proper conditioning and programming, you can control this emotion and its corresponding chemicals and responses. Realize that you can master your fear. Realize that the only obstacle in your way is yourself and how you perceive yourself.

2. <u>Rehearse</u> – Visualize how you will approach your goal or your purpose. Imagine ALL the details. What can go wrong? What can go right? What do you have control over? What is outside your control? What tools will you need... how will you get them? What people will you need to help you... how will you get them to help you? Rehearse how you will respond in these different situations. See yourself as being "OK" with any scenario... even the ones that will surprise you because you didn't think of or prepare for them. Rehearse. Rehearse. Rehearse. Rehearse until you KNOW you'll be OK with any outcome.

3. <u>Reduce</u> – Reduce your mental weight. Clear your mind of distractions and focus completely on the task at hand. Force yourself to be "in the moment". Distance yourself from people, places, and things that cause you stress or are negative to you. You cannot permit your subconscious mind to record this type of negativity. Become your own judge, jury, and executioner of your own justice system and choose who or what stays or goes. You cannot be wrong here. This is about YOU! Now is the time to have opinions. What's helping you in life? What's holding you back? What has a lot of mental weight in your life? Can you reduce its influence on you? If so, do it. The goal here is to get you thinking in terms of health, wealth, and success. Reduce your weight as much as possible. The more weight you have on your mind the more fuel (i.e., courage) you'll need to break free of your gravitational field.

4. <u>Ready</u> – Ready yourself. Prepare. Imagine. Visualize. See yourself as already having achieved your goal. How does it feel? How do you act? What tools did you have to help you achieve your goal? What are you thinking? Step outside of

yourself and view yourself objectively.  See yourself performing the action.  Get specific.  How do you look?  How do you feel at the moment of triumph?  If you can think it... you can make it happen.    Surround  yourself  with  positive  imagery  and inspirational material.  Inspiration is infectious.  Let it consume you.  Feel your ambition.  Feel your drive.  Focus on courage and  courageous  action.    Notice  that  chemical  compounds  in your body also cause these powerful and positive feelings.

5. Respond – Respond to your environment.  Respond to your feelings.  Respond to others.  Respond to yourself.  Respond to life. TAKE ACTION! Do something. Experiment. Risk. Launch yourself  out  of  your  gravitational  field.    Focus  on  Escape Velocity.   Use your moments of shrunken fear and enlarged courage to launch yourself towards your goal.  It takes many swings to chop down a tree... use the moments in your mind where you have more courage than fear to make your next big chop.  Only focus on your next swing.  Make it count!  Strike while the iron's hot.  Carpe Diem.  Jump!  Let Go! Begin! IGNITION!

6. Review – Review your action... assuming you took it.  Did it work?  Did it not?  Could your results have been better?  Could they have been worse?  Did you cause something to change? Will it be long-lasting change?  Will it be short-lived?  Are you better off with the change?  How do you feel about the action you took? Was it difficult? Were you on "autopilot"? Were you in "the Zone"?  Did you get what you were expecting?  If so, why?  If not, why not?  Would you do it again?  Will you do it again?

7. Record – Record what you have learned in a positive and firm manner.   Imprint  your  results  on  your  subconscious  mind. Repeat key thoughts and insights over and over to yourself. Use your new classical conditioning and NLP skills to improve the  efficiency  of  your  recording  process.    Believe  that  your subconscious  mind  will  attempt  to  manifest  anything  your conscious mind commands it to.  Speak positively and trustingly

to yourself.  Believe that it will make a difference.  Believe that it is changing you for the better.

8. <u>Repeat</u> – Repeat this process again... and again... and again. This process will imprint itself on your subconscious over time and with repetition.  Repetition is key.  In time, this process will become automatic and will seem effortless.  Each time you repeat it you'll gain a little more understanding and momentum, not to mention self-assurance and self-confidence. Eventually, you'll be "The One".  You'll be able to see your life and your world for what it really is and you'll be able to change things to your liking at will.  You'll have huge balls!

It is important to start small at first.  Take little bites.  Take baby steps.  Take each day at a time.  Break up your goal into smaller goals and tasks.  Make it easier to reach them.  Celebrate the little victories.  Feel success.  Build momentum.  The mindset of success helps with the next attempt.  Success breeds success.  It's the "snowball effect".  Think success. Believe success. Start confronting minor fears in your life.  Deal with them on your terms.  Allow yourself to feel victorious.  Take that feeling with you to the next challenge.

NOTICE THAT FEAR AND COURAGE ARE DICHOTOMOUS EMOTIONS. MEANING THAT THEY BOTH EXIST AT THE SAME TIME AND BATTLE EACH OTHER FOR THE DECISION-MAKING ABILITY OF YOUR MIND. NOTICE THAT THE EMOTIONS OF FEAR AND COURAGE ARE ALWAYS PRESENT IN YOUR MIND AND BODY.  IN A PERFECT WORLD, THEY WOULD EXIST IN EQUILIBRIUM WITH EACH OTHER. IN AN IMPERFECT WORLD, EITHER FEAR OR COURAGE DOMINATES YOUR MIND.  ONE FEELS GOOD... THE OTHER FEELS BAD.  THEY ARE DYNAMIC STATES OF YOUR MIND AND BODY.  CONSTANTLY SHIFTING IN ACCORDANCE TO YOUR THINKING AND PERCEPTION, CONSTANTLY DETERMINING HOW YOU WILL FEEL AND ACT.

So far, I've only talked about fear and its effect on the body. But, I've barely mentioned the opposite fear... its antidote... its mortal enemy... COURAGE.

In conclusion of this last chapter of Stage One, I want to define courage.

I believe COURAGE IS THE DECISION TO "ACT DECISIVELY" IN THE FACE OF FEAR WITH FULL KNOWLEDGE OF THE CONSEQUENCES OF SUCH ACTION; AND, THEN ACTUALLY FOLLOWING THROUGH WITH THE DECISION WITH ACTION. Dictionary.com describes the definition of "decisive" as:

1. having the power or quality of deciding; putting an end to controversy; crucial or most important: *Your argument was the decisive one.*

2. characterized by or displaying no or little hesitation; resolute; determined: *The general was known for his decisive manner.*

3. indisputable; definite: *a decisive defeat.*

4. unsurpassable; commanding: *a decisive lead in the voting.*

And, it describes the definition of "decisively" as:

1. with firmness, "'I will come along,' she said decisively"

2. with finality; conclusively; "the voting settled the argument decisively"

3. in an indisputable degree; "the Fisher Act of 1918 decisively raised their status and pay"

Being decisive is the key to enlarging courage inside you. Being decisive kills fear. It bolsters your confidence and it bolsters other people's confidence in you. Most people don't care if their leaders make the wrong decision; they just want to know their leader is capable of being and acting decisive. People want to know that their leader has a plan. And, they want to make sure their leader is sure of it. They want to know if their leader has the balls to do something with their plan. If a leader can convey that, people will follow them anywhere.

People who act decisively have balls.

If you act decisively you'll have balls.

So that's it, that's my philosophy. THINK & GROW BALLS!: How to shrink your fear and enlarge your courage.

You can do it.

In Stage Two, I'm going to tell you what to expect along the way as you practice your new skill.

# STAGE TWO

"What does not destroy me, makes me stronger." – Friedrich Nietzsche

# Feedback

"I don't measure a man's success by how high he climbs but how high he bounces when he hits bottom." – George S. Patton

## Success, Failure, & Everything In Between

In this chapter, I want to talk about something very important. I want to talk about YOUR PERCEPTION of success, failure, and every result in between. I also want to suggest a way to think about success and failure so you can shrink your fear of them. Without a doubt, if you take action and make strides towards your goal or your definite purpose, you will get responses back from your efforts. YOU WILL GET RESULTS.

Success and failure are only responses and results to your decision on whether to act or not. THEY MEAN NOTHING IN TERMS OF GOOD OR BAD. They can only mean what you perceive them to mean.

Start viewing success and failure objectively. See them for all they really are... feedback.

If you become a decisive person, you will change a lot of things about you and your environment as you see fit. Success and failure are going to happen... ALL THE TIME! Get used to them both.

Every action has an opposite and equal reaction.

You've heard this one before. It is a law of physics... of our physical world. If you change something in your life... if you take a chance... if you act, you will cause something or someone to be affected. It is impossible to avoid.

There are consequences to every action!

See these consequences as FEEDBACK.

Make it a goal to notice the specific feedback in every decision you make and every action you take. Don't worry about what the content is. Just notice what the feedback is telling you. Are you on the right path? Do I need to adjust my behavior? Was my result counterproductive to reaching my goal?

It doesn't matter if you or anyone else perceives the consequences as good or bad. Objectify them. Be indifferent to them.

Do not fear success or failure.

Profit from them both.

See them as life lessons... as learning experiences... a chance for growth.

See them as "nuggets of wisdom".

As Napoleon Hill once said:

> You are fortunate if you have learned the difference between temporary defeat and failure; more fortunate sill, if you have learned the truth that the very seed of success is dormant in every defeat that you experience.

See failure as temporary defeat, not as a total loss.

Failure is absolutely ironic. More often than not, you need the experience of a previous failure to give you the needed insight or wisdom to experience another failure. It's only after several failures do you even have the insight and wisdom you need to succeed in the first place.

In other words...

EXPERIENCE IS HUGE!

More than likely, you will never have all the information you need to make you feel completely comfortable with a potential course of action. You will need the lessons you will learn along the way. Things will be made clear to you "down the road".

Experience will come to you and it will come in the form of FEEDBACK.

Feedback can't hurt you. If it did, it would be because of your perception of it. You'd have to let it. Don't.

Just go out and get it!

You need it to succeed... EXPERIENCE WILL MAKE YOUR BALLS BIGGER.

I recommend reading biographies of famous and/or historical figures that have achieved great success (or failure). Read biographies on people such as Abraham Lincoln, Michael Jordan, Babe Ruth, Benjamin Franklin, Winston Churchill, Napoleon Bonaparte, or Thomas Edison (these folks had huge balls) and learn how many times each of them failed before achieving any notable success. Learn how they perceived failure. Try to incorporate their mindset into your own. They learned a little something from everything. They saw every failure as one step closer to their goal.

Collect materials that inspire you. Whether you're into golf, hunting, fishing, religion, technology, nature, music, or animals, you'll be able to find motivational and inspirational materials (e.g., calendars, books, CDs, mentors and coaches, etc.) that you can relate to.

**VERY IMPORTANT**

I highly recommend that you find yourself a mentor or coach to help you through your process of change and the achievement of your purpose or goal. They are invaluable as sources of wisdom, guidance, analysis, encouragement, and positive energy. I am available myself as an Escape Velocity Mentor on a limited basis. If you're interested in my services to help you dramatically increase your results and shorten the time in which you get them, don't hesitate to e-mail me at: jd@thinkandgrowballs.com

Find quotes from people you admire that inspire you. Hang them up on your wall. Put them in places where you'll see them every day.

I want to share with you some quotes on profiting from failure, overcoming adversity, and even some that deal with the fear of success to get you started:

"I have not failed. I've just found 10,000 ways that won't work." – Thomas Edison

"Ultimately, nothing much matters very much. The defeat that seems to break your heart today will be but a ripple among the waves of other experiences in the ocean of your life further ahead." – Napoleon Hill

"Sometimes a noble failure serves the world as faithfully as a distinguished success." – Edward Dowden

"Accept failure as a normal part of living. View it as part of the process of exploring your world; make a note of its lessons and move on." – Tom Hobson

"Success is going from failure to failure without losing your enthusiasm." – Winston Churchill

"Prosperity is only an instrument to be used, not a deity to be worshipped." – Calvin Coolidge

"There is something good in all seeming failures. You are not to see that now. Time will reveal it. Be patient." – Sri Swami Sivananda

"The problems of victory are more agreeable than those of defeat, but they are no less difficult." – Winston Churchill

"The majority of people meet with failure because of their lack of persistence in creating new plans to take the place of those which fail." – Napoleon Hill.

"Only those who dare to fail greatly can ever achieve greatly." – Robert Francis Kennedy

"Defeat, like a headache, warns us that something has gone wrong. If we are intelligent we look for the cause and profit by the experience." – Napoleon Hill

"Is it not strange that we fear most that which never happens? We destroy our initiative by the fear of defeat, when, in reality, defeat is a most useful tonic and should be accepted as such." – Napoleon Hill

That should be enough to get you started. In the third and final section of this e-book I list many of the quotes, sayings, and thoughts that you can use to motivate and encourage yourself. These key thoughts have helped thousands change their perspective on life and become optimistic. Some of these keys are my own thoughts and sayings that I have used to launch myself towards the next star.

Repeat these sayings to yourself as many times as you can, especially the ones you can personally relate to. Memorize them so you can recall them to yourself when you need a boost.

PROGRAM YOUR SUBCONSCIOUS MIND WITH POSITIVE THOUGHTS.

Start talking positively and "nicely" to yourself.

TELL YOURSELF THAT YOU ARE GOOD ENOUGH!

I can't emphasize that last one enough. If you believe that you are good enough to achieve and deserve the object of your desire, you will save yourself a lot of time and energy!

In the next chapter, I want to talk about what you can do when you experience failure and temporary defeat on your way to achieving your goal or purpose.

# Adjustment

"People are always blaming their circumstances for what they are. I don't believe in circumstances. The people who get on in this world are the people who get up and look for the circumstances they want, and if they can't find them, they make them." – George Bernard Shaw

## Improvement & Hitting Your Target

To begin this chapter, I want to read a few passages from the book Psycho-Cybernetics. In this book, Dr. Maxwell Maltz gives insights into the subconscious mind and how it operates as a "machine" that you can use to achieve success, health, and happiness. The following passages are very important to his philosophy:

> The new science of "Cybernetics" has furnished us with convincing proof that the so-called "subconscious mind" is not a "mind" at all, but a mechanism – a goal-striving "servo-mechanism" consisting of the brain and nervous system, which is *used by*, and *directed by* mind. The latest, and most usable concept is that man does not have two "minds," but a mind, or consciousness, which "operates" an automatic, goal-striving machine. This automatic, goal-striving machine functions very similarly to the way that electronic servo-mechanisms function, as far as basic principles are concerned, but it is much more marvelous, much more complex, that any electronic brain or guided missile ever conceived by man.

> This Creative Mechanism within you is impersonal. It will work automatically and impersonally to achieve goals of success and happiness, or unhappiness and failure, depending upon the goals which you yourself set for it. Present it with "success goals" and it functions as a "Success Mechanism." Present it with negative goals, and it operates just as impersonally, and just as faithfully as a "Failure Mechanism."

Like any other servo-mechanism, it must have a clear-cut goal, objective, or "problem" to work upon.

The goals that our own Creative Mechanism seeks to achieve are MENTAL IMAGES, or mental pictures, which we create by the use of imagination.

The key goal-image is our Self-Image.

Our Self-Image prescribes the limits for the accomplishment of any particular goals. It prescribes the "area of the possible."

Like any other servo-mechanism, our Creative Mechanism works upon information and data which we feed into it (our thoughts, beliefs, interpretations). Through our attitudes and interpretations of situations, we "describe" the problem to be worked upon.

If we feed information and data into our Creative Mechanism to the effect that we ourselves are unworthy, inferior, undeserving, incapable (a negative self-image) this data is processed and acted upon as any other data in giving us the "answer" in the form of objective experience.

Like any other servo-mechanism, our Creative Mechanism makes use of stored information, or "memory," in solving current problems and responding to current situations.

Dr. Maltz goes on to say:

Man on the other hand, has something animals haven't – Creative Imagination. Thus, man of all creatures is more than a creature, he is also a creator. With his imagination he can formulate a variety of goals. Man alone can direct his Success Mechanism by the use of imagination, or imaging ability.

We often think of "Creative Imagination" as applying only to poets, inventors, and the like. But imagination *is* creative in everything we do. Although they did not understand why, or how imagination sets our creative mechanism into action, serious thinkers of all ages, as well as hard-headed "practical" men, have recognized the fact and made use of it. "Imagination rules the world," said Napoleon. "Imagination of all man's faculties is the most God-like," said Glenn Clark. "The faculty of imagination is the great spring of human activity, and the principal source of human improvement... Destroy this faculty, and the condition of man will become as stationary as that of the brutes," said Dugold Stewart, the famous Scottish philosopher. "You can imagine your future," says Henry J. Kaiser, who attributes much of his success in business to the constructive, positive use of creative imagination.

## HOW YOUR SUCCESS MECHANISM WORKS

"You" are not a machine.

But new discoveries in the science of Cybernetics all point to the conclusion that your physical brain and nervous system make up a servo-mechanism which "You" use, and which operates very much like an electronic computer, and a mechanical goal-seeking device. Your brain and nervous system constitute a goal-striving mechanism which operates automatically to achieve a certain goal, very much as a self-aiming torpedo or missile seeks out its target and steers its way to it. Your built-in servo-mechanism functions both as a "guidance system" to automatically steer you in the right direction to achieve certain goals, or make correct responses to environment, and also as an "electronic brain" which can function automatically to solve problems, give you needed answers, and provide new ideas or "inspirations." In his book *The Computer and the Brain*, Dr. John von Newmann says that the human brain possesses the attributes of both the analogue and digital computer.

The word "Cybernetics" comes from a Greek word which means literally, "the steersman."

Servo-mechanisms are so constructed that they automatically "steer" their way to a goal, target, or "answer."

At this point, you might be asking yourself, "What the heck is a servo-mechanism?" Dr. Maltz states that there are two general types of servo-mechanisms:

Servo-mechanisms are divided into two general types: (1) where the target, goal, or "answer" is *known*, and the objective is to reach it or accomplish it, and (2) where the target or "answer" is not known and the objective is to discover or locate it. The human brain and nervous system operates in both ways.

An example of the first type is the self-guided torpedo, or the interceptor missile. The target or goal is known – an enemy ship or plane. The objective is to reach it. Such machines must "know" the target they are shooting for. They must have some sort of propulsion system which propels them forward in the general direction of the target [i.e., balls or courage]. They must be equipped with "sense organs" (radar, sonar, heat preceptors, etc.) which bring information from the target. These "sense organs" keep the machine informed when it is on the correct course (positive feedback) and when it commits an error and gets off course (negative feedback). The machine does not react or respond to positive feedback. It is doing the correct thing already and "just keeps on doing what it is doing." There must be a corrective device, however, which will respond to negative feedback. When negative feedback informs the mechanism that it is "off the beam" too far to the right, the corrective mechanism automatically causes the rudder to move so that it will steer the machine back to the left. If it "overcorrects" and heads too far to the left, this mistake is made known through negative feedback, and the corrective device moves the rudder so it will steer the machine back to the right.  The torpedo accomplishes its goal by *going forward*, *making errors*, and continually correcting them.  By a series of zigzags it literally "gropes" its way to the goal.

*Once, however, a correct or "successful response" has been accomplished – it is "remembered" for future use.  The automatic mechanism then duplicates this successful response* on future trials.  It has "learned" how to respond successfully.  It *"remembers" its successes, forgets its failures*, and repeats the successful action without any further conscious "thought" – or as a habit.

Now let us suppose that the room is dark so you cannot see pack of gum.  You know, or hope, the gum is on the table, along with a variety of other objects.  Instinctively, your hand will begin to "grope" back and forth, performing zigzag motions (or "scanning") rejecting one object after another, until the gum is found and "recognized."  This is an example of the second type of servo-mechanism.  Recalling a name temporarily forgotten is another example.  A "Scanner" in your brain scans back through your stored memories until the correct name is "recognized."  An electronic brain solves problems in much the same way.  First of all, a great deal of data must be fed into the machine.  This stored, or recorded information is the machine's "memory."  A problem is posed to the machine.  It scans back through its memory until it locates the only "answer" which is consistent with and meets all the conditions of the problem.  Problem and answer together constitute a "whole" situation or structure (the problem) is given to the machine, it locates the only missing "parts," or the right size brick, so to speak, to complete the structure.

This is a fascinating book (and one that I recommend you read) that addresses a central issue to both Napoleon Hill's *Think & Grow Rich* philosophy and my philosophy on *Think & Grow Balls!*... THAT YOUR MIND IS EITHER TRYING TO FIGURE OUT WHAT THE TARGET IS OR IT IS TRYING TO ACHIEVE, OBTAIN, OR REACH IT.

This is why it is so important to know your definite purpose, your mission, or set goals for yourself. If you don't, your mind will be zigzagging back and forth in the dark continually asking yourself, "Is this it... is this it... is this it?" If you do know what your goals are, your mind will be zigzagging TOWARDS it.

In other words, YOUR MIND WORKS MORE EFFICIENTLY WHEN YOU KNOW WHAT YOUR TARGET IS.

Your subconscious and central nervous system and your "success mechanism" can all be employed to reach your goal... to achieve your dreams.

It will help to remember the analogy of the heat-seeking missile used to describe the power of our conscious and subconscious mind in programming and conditioning ourselves to achieve our dreams.

THE JOURNEY OF ACHIEVING YOUR DREAMS IS JUST ONE OVER-CORRECTION AFTER ANOTHER AS YOU ZIGZAG TOWARDS YOUR TARGET. IT DOES NOT MATTER HOW FAR AWAY THE TARGET IS OR HOW MANY TIMES YOU OVER-CORRECT AND ZIGZAG. THE ONLY THING THAT MATTERS IS THAT YOU HIT THE TARGET.

To simplify this metaphor even further:

FAILURE IS JUST FEEDBACK TELLING YOU THAT YOU'RE NOT ON TRACK TO HIT YOUR TARGET. IT IS MERELY A SIGNAL TELLING YOU TO CORRECT YOUR MOVEMENT BACK TOWARDS YOUR GOAL.

If you fail, all you need to do is make an adjustment.

If you fail again, adjust again.

Keep adjusting until you hit your target.

Keep improving until you hit your target.

Keep adjusting until you reach your goals.

Keep improving until you reach your goals.

Keep adjusting until you achieve the life of your dreams.

Keep improving.

The previous chapter explains that every time you take action in your life you will receive feedback and that, when looked at objectively, is neither "good" nor "bad".

This chapter explains that feedback, when viewed as either positive or negative, works as a guiding mechanism for our conscious and subconscious mind. And, that if you adjust your actions, if you continually improve, you will eventually hit your target.

In the next and final chapter of this e-book, I will teach you about being "in the zone", being "The One", being on "autopilot", the end result of classical conditioning, programming, and practice.

I'll teach you about the process of mastery.

# Autopilot

"What are you trying to tell me... that I can dodge bullets?" asked Neo.
"No, Neo... I'm trying to tell you that when you're ready, you won't have to," replied Morpheus. – *The Matrix*

## Believing & Mastery

Have you ever been driving in your car and suddenly realized that you cannot remember exactly how you arrived at your current location?  Most people have.  What's surprising, is that if you think about all the decisions and complex movements that are required to drive your car to a destination (e.g., turning the wheel properly, applying pressure to the accelerator and brake with your right foot, depressing the clutch with your left, shifting gears, using your turn signals, windshield wipers, etc.) you can understand how amazing your conscious and subconscious minds are.  When you first started learning how to drive, you had to think of everything!  It probably took a lot of practice.  Eventually, however, the process of driving became easier and more comfortable as your skill improved.  Now, as you have many years and miles behind the wheel, your mind is able to wander while you drive.  Your mind can solve all the problems of the world while your subconscious mind sends all the required signals to the muscles of your body at just the right times to get you to your destination safely.  In fact, nowadays people can (usually) drink a beverage, eat, smoke, actively talk and listen, talk on a cell phone, apply makeup, shave, read, sing, pick their nose, and I've even heard a story about people that change their clothes all while they're driving. (Yes... actually change their clothes!  Can someone help me figure out how you do that one?)

How is this possible?

How can something as difficult and complex as driving become so easy and mundane?

It's possible because you are on "autopilot".

You're in the "zone".

Basically, driving has become a conditioned habit for you. You have driven so much that your "style" of driving is imprinted in your subconscious mind... you no longer need to think about everything involved. Driving has become automatic for you.

How can "autopilot" or "being in the zone" be described? Although, I believe this state of mind to be relative to the person experiencing it, the state of mind known as "autopilot" or "being in the zone" can be generally defined by as:

1. Having an extraordinary degree of self-acceptance and self-trust.

2. Having an ability to remain detached from what is going on around you.

3. Knowing ourselves and accepting your limitations.

4. Having the capacity for vivid appreciativeness – a childlike quality of seeing something new or good in almost every experience.

5. Being totally absorbed in the task at hand.

6. Having clear goals.

7. Letting go of control but, paradoxically, exercising control of your thoughts and emotions.

8. Losing yourself in the task, not feeling self-conscious.

9. Not worrying about the consequences of your performance.

10.    Having the ability to go with the flow so your performance seems simple and easy and is never impaired or rushed by a flood of thoughts.

Now, try to think of some other difficult and complex activities that can be done on autopilot or in the zone.

How about playing a musical instrument?

What about playing sports?

What about cooking, gardening, and other hobbies?

Try to think of some others that are specific to you. List a couple of activities that were difficult at first but now you no longer even need to concentrate on them in order for you to successfully complete them.

I've got one for you...

How about thinking, feeling, and acting decisively and courageously?

Is it possible that shrinking your fear and enlarging your courage is a skill?

Can you condition yourself to control your fear, quiet your mind, and calm your body so you can make decisive decisions and act on them when you need to... each and every time?

Sure you can...

What do you think military boot camp is for?

What do you think driver's education is supposed to accomplish.

What do you think music and sports practice does for these skills?

That's right... they all prepare your subconscious mind to respond in a favorable manner so that you can perform under stress and without consciously thinking about it.

Is acting decisively a skill?

Is "having balls" and using them a skill?

Is it possible that you could practice "having balls" so much that you start to think, feel, and act decisively without even realizing that you're doing it?

I think it is... and that's the message of the final chapter of this e-book.

You can condition, reprogram, and affirm your subconscious mind to master your fear and launch yourself toward the life of your dreams.

You can Think & Grow Balls!

You can live life to the fullest!

You can have the life of your dreams!

You MUST realize that it is possible for YOU!

If you've seen the movie *The Matrix*, how can you forget the scene during the climax of the movie where after being shot and killed by Agent Smith, Neo resurrects himself and finally, for the first time, realizes that he IS The One and literally sees the matrix for what it truly is... something that is totally under his control!

What follows is one of the most powerful movie sequences I've ever scene. In fact, just as I'm writing this, I've got goose bumps and the hair on my arms is standing on end. (That was my conscious mind triggering a subconscious response that caused my brain and body to produce and release adrenaline, by the way.)

Realize for yourself that you can be "The One".

Choose your goals and your targets.

Practice the Eight R's:

1. Realize
2. Rehearse
3. Reduce
4. Ready
5. Respond
6. Review
7. Record
8. Repeat

Practice them until you become a master on shrinking your fear and enlarging your courage.

Launch yourself toward the life of your dreams!

I know you can do it!

THINK & GROW BALLS!

# STAGE THREE

"The individual has always had to struggle to keep from being overwhelmed by the tribe. If you try it, you will be lonely often, and sometimes frightened. But no price is too high to pay for the privilege of owning yourself." – Friedrich Nietzsche

# Powerful Thoughts & Beliefs

"What you want to be eventually, that you must be every day; and by and by the quality of your deeds will get down into your soul." – Napoleon Hill

## Inspiration & Thoughts to Live By

This last section of this e-book is really an appendix. In writing this, I came across so many pieces of good advice, quotes, sayings, and thoughts that I had a difficult time deciding which ones to use. I chose the best ones (in my opinion) for the headings of each chapter and used others in the actual text. This section is for all the ones that were good and important, but didn't make the final cut.

Some of these quotes are my own material but most of them are from other people whom I admire. In some cases, I wasn't able to remember the quotes word for word so I did the best I could at paraphrasing them. In other cases, I knew the quote but didn't know who said it. Basically, I tried my best to give credit where credit is due.

So let's take a look at some of them:

Power is 80 percent taken and 20 percent given.

"One for the money, two for the show; three to get ready, and four to go!" – chanted by children on playgrounds as they prepare to launch themselves from the swing set at its highest point.

If you let the way people think of you influence the way you act... you've already lost.

"Confidence is not jumping out of a perfectly good airplane with a parachute on your back... that's bravery. Confidence is saying 'See you at the bottom.'" – Mystery

"When you get into a tight place and everything goes against you, 'til it seems as though you could not hold on a minute longer, never give up then, for that is just the place and time that the tide will turn." – Harriet Beecher Stowe

"All you are or ever shall become is the result of the use to which you put your mind." – Napoleon Hill

"Every failure is a blessing in disguise, providing it teaches some needed lesson one could not have learned without it.  Most so-called failures are only temporary defeats." – Unknown

"A good encyclopedia contains most of the known facts of the world, but they are as useless as sand dunes until organized and expressed in terms of action." – Unknown

"Do not "tell" the world what you can do… show it!" – Unknown

"Yes, he succeeded… but he almost failed!"  So did Robert Fulton and Abraham Lincoln and nearly all the others whom we call successful. No man ever achieved worthwhile success who did not, at one time or other, find himself with at least one foot hanging well over the brink of failure.

"You can always become the person you would have liked to be." – Unknown

"The only man who makes no mistakes is the man who never does anything.  Do not be afraid of mistakes, providing you do not make the same one twice." – Theodore Roosevelt

Careful analysis of 178 men who are known to be successful disclosed the fact that all had failed many times before arriving.

"They say that time changes things, but you actually have to change them yourself." – Andy Warhol

"Begin now – not tomorrow, not next week, but today – to seize the moment and make this day count.  Remember, yesterday is gone and tomorrow may never come." – Ellen Kreidman

"There's no harm in trying.
Nothing can harm you until it comes.
And it may never come.
And if it does it may be something else again.
And those who say they'll try anything once,
Often try nothing twice, three times,
Arriving late at the gate of dreams worth dying for."
- Carl Sandburg, from the poem *Breathing Tokens*

"Destiny is not a matter of chance; it is a matter of choice.  It is not a thing to be waited for; it is a thing to be achieved." – William Jennings Bryan

"I know I am here.  I know I had nothing to do with my coming, and I shall have but little, if anything, to do with my going.  Therefore I will not worry because worries are of no avail." – Unknown

"The lucky or successful person has learned a simple secret.  Call up, capture, evoke the feeling of success.  When you feel successful and self-confident, you will act successfully." – Maxwell Maltz

"Peak performers are people who approach any set of circumstances with the attitude that they can get it to turn out the way they want it to.  Not once in a while.  Regularly.  They can count on themselves." – Charles Garfield

"The man who actually knows just what he wants in life has already gone a long way toward attaining it." – Unknown

"The heights by great men reached and kept were not attained by sudden flight, but they, while their companions slept, were toiling upward in the night." – Henry Wadsworth Longfellow

"Find something you love to do and you'll never have to work a day in your life." – Harvey Mackay

"Victory comes only after many struggles and countless defeats... each rebuff is an opportunity to move forward; turn away from them, avoid them, and you throw away your future." – Og Mandino

"The mind that made you sick can also make you well." – Unknown

"We are what we think. All that we are arises with our thoughts. With our thoughts we make the world." – Buddha

"You are a product of your environment. So choose the environment that will best develop you toward your objective... are the things around you helping you toward success – or are they holding you back?" – W. Clement Stone

"Sometimes the subconscious mind manifests a wisdom several steps or even years ahead of the conscious mind, and has its own way of leading us toward our destiny." – Nathaniel Branden

"As I grow older I pay less attention to what men say. I just watch what they do." – Andrew Carnegie

"In any moment of decision the best thing you can do is the right thing, the next best thing is the wrong thing, and the worst thing you can do is nothing." – Theodore Roosevelt

"There are no limitations to the mind except those we acknowledge." – Unknown

"Both poverty and riches are the offspring of thought." – Napoleon Hill

"I think I can... I think I can... I think I can." – *The Little Engine That Could*

"If you want to be a leader... then lead!" – Unknown

Actions speak louder than words.

Fake it 'til you make it.

Act as if.

Change your perception of the world... change the world.

Perception precedes reality.

Assume complete responsibility for your own life.

It's only important if you make it important.

Life makes life better for life.

The quickest way to screw up your own life is to hang around people who already have.

Life is hazardous to your health.

"Attitude determines altitude." – Unknown

"A good rule of thumb to go by is if you have more than one option, method, or direction you can take, choose the most difficult of all the possible choices.  The harder it is, the more likely you are to fail quicker.  And, when you get back up to try again, you're likely to fail again (just don't fail the same way... after all, the definition of an idiot is someone that keeps doing the same things and expects different results) and that's good.  Learn from your mistakes and choose to see them as a necessary step towards accomplishment. Nothing good in life comes easy and when you have reached your goal by taking the difficult path, you will have more wisdom, self-confidence, and balls than anyone who chose an easier option to get to the same destination.  You may not always succeed by taking the most difficult path; know this.  Take pride in the fact that you had the balls to attempt what most would not.  Even in failure, you succeed in gaining wisdom, but YOU MUST CHOOSE TO THINK THAT WAY." – Yours Truly

"God helps those who help themselves." – Unknown

Give yourself permission

Every day in every way, my balls are getting bigger and bigger.

"I don't regret anything I've ever done.  I regret immensely the things I never did." – Yours Truly

"I may never pass this way again." – Unknown

# Ounce of Difference
## Ten Commandments of Leadership, Service, and Growth

1. People are illogical, unreasonable, and self-centered. Love them anyway.

2. If you do good, people will accuse you of selfish, ulterior motives. Do good anyway.

3. If you are honest, some people will laugh at you. Be honest anyway.

4. If you speak out for what you believe in, people will make fun of you. Speak out anyway.

5. Think big and small-minded people will sneer at you. Think big anyway.

6. What you spend years building may be destroyed overnight. Build anyway.

7. People are crying out for help but may attack you if you help them. Help them anyway.

8. Some days there won't be a song in your heart. Sing anyway.

9. The world loves top dogs. Fight for a few underdogs anyway.

10. Give the world the best you have and most people will not even notice. Give this miraculous, fragile world the best you have anyway.

# The End

Thank you very much for purchasing and reading this e-book. If you'd like to send me some feedback, please do so. If you do, please be as specific as you can to help me understand what you liked or didn't like. This e-book, like most things, is a work in progress and I may use your suggestions in future works. Also, by sending me a message, you authorize me to use it in future material, if I so choose. You can send me an e-mail to my personal address:

jd@thinkandgrowballs.com